WINDOWS TO NATURE

A Book for Teachers of Children from 3 to 8 Years of Age

by MILDRED MASHEDER

Illustrations by
Susanna Vermaase

*To George, aged seven, who has given me
some good ideas.*

Published by WWF UK, Panda House,
Weyside Park, Catteshall Lane, Godalming,
Surrey GU7 1XR, UK.

Designed by: Schermuly Design Co, London.
Printed by: The Richmond Publishing Co. Ltd.
Illustrations by: Susanna Vermaase.

ISBN: 0 947613 38 2

ACKNOWLEDGEMENTS

My special thanks to Damian Randle, Editor of Green
Teacher; to Richard Yarwood, infant teacher in
Haringey; to Margery Mitchell, Lecturer in Environmental Studies at the London Montessori College, and
to the many practising nursery and infant teachers,
who have given me the benefit of their experience
and successfully carried out many of the activities
described in this book.

CONTENTS

INTRODUCTION

This book sets out to do two things: to encourage children of nursery and infant age groups to learn about and enjoy the wonders of the natural world, and to lay the foundations for them to develop responsible attitudes to the care and protection of the world in which they live. The approach is activity based, with practical suggestions for hands-on experiments and exploration of the natural world.

The sequence of chapters follows the natural development of the children, from the personal to the social, from their immediate environment to the community and then on to the wider world. It is recommended that all children follow this sequence, adding systematically to their experience and knowledge in the form of a spiral curriculum.

The introductory chapters are suitable for all age groups. Through a variety of games and activities, designed to improve confidence and self-esteem, the children are encouraged to learn to trust one another, to express their feelings and to explore the power of their senses. Examples of co-operative play and collaborative work offer opportunities to explore social development.

These two chapters form the background to the practical activities in the rest of the book, which encourage the personal creativity of individual children at the same time as enabling them to work harmoniously together.

If children are to be able to convey their ideas and feelings about the natural world, they need to use the full range of their creative faculties, so the third chapter explores how to build up deeper understanding and knowledge, through such media as drama, music, dance, painting, sculpture and photography.

Chapter four introduces the practical work in school. It begins with ideas for growing things, studying animal and plant life in the classroom, and extends to include projects concerned with the improvement of the school environment, from bird tables and ponds to habitats for wildlife.

Next, we encourage children to explore how the local community can help to provide a healthier and more beautiful environment. By building up a clearer picture of the environmental needs of the locality, they can develop a sense of responsibility towards their community and realise that they too can contribute to making it a nicer place to live in. Two kinds of visits are dealt with in more detail: botanic gardens and city farms. The activities suggested could be adapted to other places of interest in your area.

Chapter six helps children to put their experiences of the natural world into the perspective of the interdependence of all things. Simple role play activities help young children appreciate that we are all a part of a much larger scheme of things. Older children can begin to learn about the harm people can inflict on the natural order of things: for example, acid rain, the greenhouse effect and the threat to the ozone layer. The younger age group need to familiarise themselves with the properties of the physical world by doing the various explorative activities in preparation for an understanding of the complexities that lie ahead.

Chapter seven further explores the concept of interdependence, focusing in particular on food chains and habitats. Children are asked to think about their own habitat and compare their needs with those of other living things. Three regions are then chosen to illustrate changes that affect the whole balance of nature: the temperate forests, the plains areas and the tropical rainforests. Questions posed include "What is happening to them?", "What effects does this have?" and "What can we do about it?"

Chapter eight is concerned with the threat to wildlife. Younger children can be expected to gain more knowledge of and empathy towards the species they are studying. Older children could act out simple role plays and find out what action is being taken to save endangered plants and animals.

LINKS WITH THE NATIONAL CURRICULUM

Environmental education as a cross-curricular theme embraces all aspects of the National Curriculum.

It should provide opportunities for children to acquire the knowledge, skills, attitudes, commitment and values needed to protect and improve the environment.

It should also arouse pupils' awareness and curiosity about the environment and encourage active participation in resolving environmental problems.

The activities in this book go some way towards meeting these and many other requirements, covering attainment targets in Key Stage 1 as well as preparing older children for the first levels of Key Stage 2.

In Science, children should be encouraged to observe and explore the natural world, posing questions, designing experiments, testing, recording and classifying. Many of the investigations suggested follow this approach.

There are a number of opportunities for practice in mathematical skills, from measuring rainfall and sorting leaf shapes to constructing and interpreting block graphs.

Considerable emphasis is placed on language, with children inventing simple role-play situations, producing pieces to writing, following instructions and participating as speakers and listeners in group activities. Drama is often used to convey more complex concepts.

Attainment targets in Design and Technology are also covered, whether it be devising questionnaires about playgrounds, recording different designs for a mini-greenhouse, making a kite, a windmill, an animal mask or an animal enclosure.

Through pursuing the ideas in this book, children will also gain a historical perspective on the world around them, growing to appreciate the enormous changes which have taken place this century and the impact of human activities.

Many of the themes lend themselves naturally to geographical studies. In their locality, children are encouraged to plan nature trails, school gardens and wildlife areas and contribute generally to improving the quality of their environment. Their awareness of the world beyond their area is enhanced by research, discussions and painting.

Art activities offer young children the opportunity to express their feelings about the natural world and explore the full potential of their creative powers. Music is introduced through links with the sounds of nature, and physical education is incorporated into work on the body as well as co-operative games.

Religious festivals all over the world celebrate nature and the seasons, and the idea of loving others is the foundation of most faiths. The central theme throughout this book is caring - caring for other human beings and for all living things.

CHAPTER I

PERSONAL DEVELOPMENT

AFFIRMATION AND A GOOD SELF-CONCEPT

It is only when children feel good about themselves that they can begin to feel good about other people and things. This self-concept will be reflected in their whole outlook and attitude towards the natural world.

There are many activities and games that will help build confidence and self-esteem. Here is just a selection.

If I were an animal: In a circle, each child names the type of animal (or plant) that they would like to be and gives the reason why. Remember that this must be a positive exercise. (You may prefer to save games that need knowledge of nature until the children have experienced a number of the activities in this book.)

Initials: Can children think of an animal or plant that has the same initials as them? For example, Tom the Tiger, Mary the Monkey. Younger ones can go by the sound, eg George the Giraffe.

My Name: What do they like about their name? If they would like a different one, which would they choose and why?

Complimentary Adjectives: Can children think of an adjective that says something good or amusing about themselves? For older children, make it a word that begins with the same letter as their name: Lovely Lucy, Jolly Jim, Happy Hannah.

Friendly Wheel: Ask the children about some of the things that people have done for them that made them feel good or special. Make a large cardboard wheel and divide it into sections, writing a friendly action in each one, using suggestions given by the children. Cut an arrow out of coloured card and fasten it to the centre of the circle with a round clip. The children can spin the wheel and try to do what it tells them, for example "Help a classmate", "Pick

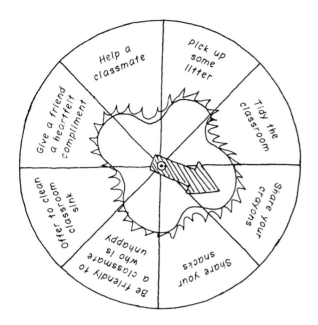

up some litter", "Tidy the classroom", "Share your crayons".

Wanted: Let the class make "Wanted" posters using photographs or drawings done by a partner. They should give details of appearance and hobbies. It is best if each child makes their own poster or if the exercise is done in pairs.

Guess Who?: Write everyone's name on pieces of paper. In small groups, the children take it in turns to pick out a name and describe the person in a positive way. The rest have to guess who it is.

"Me" Books: The children can make their own books about "Me", including photos and pictures of themselves, friends, family and pets. Stories can include: "My life story", "My biggest adventure", "The best day I ever had", "The worst day", "Something I have grown or looked after", "A place I like going to", "A secret place where I can hide".

Finger Prints: Make a pad of sponge soaked in washable ink. Each child puts both thumbs on the ink, pressing well from side to side, and prints them on a piece of clean paper or in their "Me" book. This is proof of how unique each child is - no two sets of fingerprints are the same.

Getting to Know Each Other: The children find out from each other one thing that they have in common and then go on to the next one. It might be colour, clothes, likes or dislikes. They could use a tape recorder and act out an interview situation.

Rogues Gallery: Have a class gallery of portraits. How will the children frame their photographs? One way is to cut out two similar rectangles of card 6 cm larger than the photograph all the way round. How can they measure this? Put the photo in the middle, draw round it and cut out an opening a little smaller than the photo. Young children may need help with this. Glue the bottom and sides of the card together, making sure that the bottom is joined just below the cut-out part, so that the snapshot will not slip down

to the bottom. Cut out a wedge of card to prop the frame up. Fold it over and stick it down at the top so that the wide edge is level with the bottom of the card.

Mirror, Mirror: If it is possible to bring a full length mirror into the classroom, get the children to draw themselves one at a time. It helps if the mirror has a thin masking of tape dividing the reflection into three parts. Alternatively, partners could draw each other life size. Class Self-Esteem: In small groups, devise a logo or symbol to represent the class and print it on old plain T-shirts.

- Make a class banner with the symbol as the main motif.

- Hold a class hobby exhibition.

- Make a class scrapbook with everyone contributing.

- Start up a class newspaper, radio station with a tape recorder, and even a class satellite TV channel!

- Make a class mural of "What I Like Doing" with cut-outs from magazines.

Sensitivity should of course be shown towards children who experience genuine difficulty in thinking of positive ways of describing themselves. This may be indicative of more serious problems and should be handled appropriately.

FAMILIES

Any discussion about families should be at the teacher's discretion. Great sensitivity and caution should be used, bearing in mind adopted children, single parent families and bereavements. Most young children enjoy talking about their families and this can be an affirming exercise. But, what do they know about animal families or plant families? How alike and how different are they from human families?

We sometimes talk of the world as a family of nations and children can be introduced to the concept of interdependence through activities that show how each family is dependent on its individual members. Similarly, as nations, we all depend on each other to care for our planet. Later the children can build up a picture of the interdependence of all living things in web form.

Family Groups: Brainstorm different kinds of family groups who help each other: father, mother and children; step-parents and children; single parent families; couples without children; and various computations with grandparents, aunts, uncles and cousins. Ask them about their families and relations. What do they do to help one another? What do the children do to help them? Are neighbours important to the family? In what ways?

Family Trees: See if they can find out about their grandparents, uncles, aunts and cousins and make a simple family tree with drawings.

World Maps: If you have children whose families come from different countries , put little flags or name tags on a map of the world to show the countries concerned. You might invite the parents to come in and tell the class what they know or recall of their country of origin. It might only be grandparents who can recount experiences first-hand, but many families go back to their native countries for holidays.

Family Photographs: Some children could make their own photo albums and insert or stick in photos of the family. In the same way, they could make a class book of the pupils engaged in various co-operative activities, thus creating the sense of the class as a family. The book could record all the different ways in which the class has contact with nature.

Family Names: Where did the children's names come from? Can they think of names that originated from the work people did, for example, Miller, Smith, Baker, Carter, Brewer, Tailor? Some people have names from the place where they lived, like Jack London, and some from their fathers, like Johnson or Jackson.

Animal Families: See if the children can find out about families or animals that help each other. For example, female lions work with their sisters and their offspring to catch their prey; female elephants live together as a group, protecting their young.

Birthdays: Every member of the class should have a special day, usually their birthday, but for those whose birthdays occur in the holidays or at weekends another time should be chosen. The children could brainstorm various ways to celebrate: a giant card; a birthday hat or crown; sweets to be made that need no cooking (peppermint creams, marzipan dates); a lucky dip basket with everyone contributing a small gift at the beginning of the school year. An outline of the celebrating child can be traced on wallpaper with everyone writing something new and positive that they have discovered about him or her.

TRUST

Everyone in the class needs to build up faith in themselves, in their teacher and their classmates. An atmosphere of affirmation and trust in the classroom will help to give the security in personal relationships that every child needs. This security is the keynote to approaching new experiences and learning with confidence and enthusiasm.

Making a Blindfold: Trust activities rely a great deal on blindfolds, so it would be a good idea for every child to make one. They could plan how to do it and discuss which materials would be best to use. Will they be fixed with elastic or tied at the back? The children would need to measure their heads. Do their blindfolds work? Do they fit?

Blind Trust: The class divides into two equal groups and one group is blindfolded. The seeing group all choose a partner and lead them around for five minutes. If possible this should be out of the classroom and into the school grounds. The idea is for the guide to take great care of the partner, making sure that he or she does not bump into anyone or anything.

Once they can do this, the guides can lead them to feel natural things - stones, soils, plants, flowers; and different textures - smooth, rough, slimy, silky. A favourite game is to lead the partner to a special spot or a tree and then, taking a tortuous route back, get them to find their way back by feeling the clues that they touched. The other partner then has a turn, and after each session the children can talk freely about how they felt. Did they feel afraid and helpless, or were they quite happy about being led? What did the guides feel? A variation of this activity is for one partner to act as a guide dog.

Trust Modelling: Place a ball of clay on a table between two children who are blindfolded. The challenge is for them to create a form together. It's best for them to agree on something beforehand, such as a particular animal.

THE FIVE SENSES

Consciousness of nature is developed and enhanced by our awareness of the five senses. Observation is not merely through seeing, but also hearing, touching, smelling and tasting. Young children often observe more closely than adults, and we can encourage their awareness by means of experiments, games, explorations and investigations. Sometimes, people talk about their "sixth sense" - when they just feel intuitively that something is right or wrong, for example. Have the children ever had that feeling? All good scientists and artists combine their powers of observation with creative intuition and this process cannot be nurtured too early.

THE SENSE OF SIGHT

Throughout this book there is an emphasis on the recognition of plants and animals by their names and characteristics; children do like to know what things are called and this need not detract from their enjoyment of nature, as long as they are not pressured into it.

Nature Spot: Divide the class into small groups and prepare a tray for each group with a variety of nature specimens. Show the tray to the children for half a minute and then cover it and have a group brainstorm to recall as many of the items as possible. Make a list of them, with drawings or symbols for those children who are not yet reading, and then uncover to reveal those missed out. A further activity can be to add an accurate description to each one: red leaf, bare twig, soft feather, winged seed. For older children names

of leaves of trees that they have studied could be asked for: oak, laurel, beech, plane, horse chestnut. If flowers are used for this or any other activity, they should be picked very sparingly from the school grounds or the children's homes; leaves can usually be found at the foot of each tree. Never pick wild flowers. In this way, we set an example to children, and encourage them to show respect for all growing things.

Magnifying Glasses and Binoculars: Working in pairs, children could use a magnifying glass to examine plants or creatures, observing their characteristics and recording them. They may need to practise focusing on their subject. They could then try using binoculars, first viewing still objects at a distance and focusing accurately, then progressing to focus on living creatures, like birds on the bird table and, if possible, capturing them in flight. By looking through the different ends of the binoculars, they should understand that one end will make things distant and small, while the other makes them close-to and large.

Microscopes: Children can examine plant material through a microscope: leaf veins, flower petals, stamens covered with pollen, seeds, fungi. They can look at a drop of pond water and see tiny creatures and vegetation. They should record their findings with drawings to show magnification.

THE SENSE OF HEARING

What do I hear?: Tape a series of familiar sounds and get the children to identify them, for example, a typewriter, a dog barking, the school bell, a door banging, the rustle of leaves as you walk through them, the flow of water from a tap. Older children can tape their own choice of sounds, working in small groups.

Animal Sounds: Older children could make a tape of animal sounds, from their pets or on a visit to a farm or zoo. The tapes could be used in pairs with each child in turn identifying the sounds. Can the children imitate the sounds? Volunteers could perform one at a time and the others could guess the animal. They could then devise their own sounds with percussion instruments to imitate animal noises.

Bird Song: Play a cassette with named bird songs for the children. (British Wild Birds No RMC4008 from the BBC Shop, Henry Wood House, Nos 4 & 5 Langham Place, Upper Regent Street, London W1A 1AA or from any large retail shop, would be suitable to use.) After repeating it several times, see if they can tell which song is being replayed. This can be preparation for a nature walk or walk in the school grounds. Older children can make their own tape recordings of bird song: thrushes, robins and blackbirds are particularly clear.

Voices of Nature: When you're out on a nature walk or in the school grounds, ask everyone to stop what they"re doing for a minute, be quite still and listen to the rustle of grasses in the wind, the sounds of bees or the songs of birds. These sounds could be the inspiration for **very** simple poems or a piece of creative writing. The class could first brainstorm and list nature sound words: eg. buzzing, chirping, twittering, blowing, singing, barking, rustling, and link them with the creatures concerned: for example, "Bees buzzing", "Mice squeaking", "Trees rustling in the breeze".

Sounds of the Countryside: As a preparation or follow-up to a visit to the countryside, play the tape "Birds and Sounds of the Countryside" No ZCM299 from the BBC shop (address above). There are many habitats represented including farms, fields, hedge-rows, wetlands, sea coast, broadleafed woods, pine forest, mountains and moorland.

Pomander: Cover an orange with cloves, set really close together. (Younger children would find a tangerine easier.) Dry it thoroughly and thread a ribbon through it to hang in the classroom. Poman-ders make welcome presents to hang in wardrobes.

Perfumed Path: Take the children on a walk in the school grounds or a park, or ideally in the countryside, and look for plants that are perfumed, or have a distinctive odour. When they have completed the walk, each child takes their partner (designated beforehand) to introduce them to the various scents they have come across.

THE SENSE OF SMELL

THE SENSE OF TASTE

What's in the Bag?: Make little bags full of natural objects that have a distinctive smell: lavender, mint, tangerine, onion, curry powder, and see if the children can guess what is inside. Older children can make their own bags and decide what to fill them with. They can be made into small gifts tied with coloured ribbon.

Herb Planting: Herbs can be cultivated from seed in pots or window boxes and later in the school garden. Pinch a leaf and say which one it is: basil, mint, rosemary, thyme.

Blindfold Tasting: (SAFETY NOTE: Warn children not to taste - or smell - anything without asking an adult.) There are various categories that could be chosen for tasting sessions: fruit, fresh and dried: apple, pear, orange, grape, blackberry, tangerine; currants, sultanas, raisins, cherries, dried apricots, peel; salads: tomato, cucumber, lettuce, cabbage, radish, avocado, celery, carrot; drinks: orange, grape-fruit, pineapple, apple, blackcurrant. After each tast-ing, children should describe their observations and

identify differences, for example, between oranges and tangerines, currants and sultanas, lettuce and cabbage, freshly squeezed orange juice and orange-ade. They could distinguish between various powders: cocoa, milk, flour, icing sugar. In some cases they could look at the powders first and try to guess what they are, then rely on taste to distinguish them: for example, caster sugar and salt, white flour, icing sugar and sherbet. Older children might think of other tests to identify them. Would flour dissolve in water? Which powder might fizz in water?

Each tasting should be recorded and descriptions noted, including comparisons. The tastings could be in categories or mixed and older children could list them according to their criteria, making sub-divisions where possible: citrus fruit, root or leafy vegetables. Alternatively, the food could be listed in terms of taste: sweet, sour, bland, sharp, fizzy.

THE SENSE OF TOUCH

Lucky Dip: Put a number of small objects in a bucket filled with packing chips or torn-up pieces of paper and get the children, one at a time, to explore an item through their sense of touch and identify it, taking it out to check. Larger objects could be put in a pillow case. Most teachers will be familiar with the feeling activity where the children sit in a circle with a blanket covering their hands. Objects are then passed round one at a time with an imaginative story to accompany them. The teacher can initiate the story and then it can be continued by each child in turn as they receive the item destined for them. These three versions can all be used to develop descriptive vocabulary: adjectives like smooth, prickly, spongy, rough, slippery. To link this to the environment, the objects should be natural ones, for example, a feather, an acorn, a conker, a shell, a pebble or a "Litterbug" saga with various tins, plastic cups, polyurethene containers, banana peel or potato peelings in a plastic bag, an old newspaper, a milk bottle, a beer bottle, a wine bottle, a battery in a plastic bag (gloves to be worn). The stories created might turn out to be somewhat nonsensical, but these are ways to give free play to the imagination.

Touching and Textures: Each pair of children has a shoe box in which to collect as many different textures as possible: hard, soft, prickly, smooth, dry, slimy, rough, spongy, fuzzy. This could be done in the school grounds or on a nature walk. Each pair chooses criteria to sort. They then classify their objects and explain their classification to the rest of

the class. Older children could sort them according to different criteria, for example, those that have two attributes in common: rough and hard, smooth and shiny. A list of all the words describing touch could be displayed and form the basis of creative writing about their finds.

MY FIVE SENSES BOOK

Discuss any ideas they have about what they would include in such a book and then get them to design their own.

One way is to make a book of holed A4 paper and tie the pages together with ribbon or coloured string. The title page could be decorated to illustrate the five senses in some way and each page could deal with a different sense:

The Seeing Page: The child draws a picture of an eye and then a picture of themselves or one that they like to look at. Glue in a piece of tinfoil to act as a mirror.

The Hearing Page: Pictures could include: an ear, musical instruments, a guitar with a rubber band stapled to it, so that it can be plucked.

The Smelling Page: Draw a nose and then glue on to the paper a variety of different materials that have distinctive smells: for example, pressed thyme or mint, coffee, cloves, perfume on a piece of cotton wool.

The Touching Page: The child draws a picture of their hand or traces round it and then chooses different textures to glue on to this page: fur, a tiny shell, foil, cotton wool.

The Tasting Page: Draw a tongue and then glue on to the page samples of salt, sugar, cocoa. (Use tiny measuring spoons to allocate each portion to each child.) Reference: Aliki, "My Five Senses", NY Crowell, 1972.

MEMORIES OF THE SENSES

Does a certain scent, sound, taste or touch remind children of a time when they were especially happy? It might be the smell of cakes being baked for a birthday party or the feel of snow on hands and face. Can they describe their experiences? The children's contributions could inspire a group poem, listing

each memory as adjectives and nouns and each line keeping to a simple rhythm.

Animal Senses: Do some animals have specially developed senses? Children can use reference books to find out.

Sight: Birds of prey and insects can see better than we can. Many have compound eyes, like flies and dragon flies; otters see clearly under water; tigers see like humans in the daylight, but seven times more acutely in the dark. Why do they have such good sight?

Hearing: Which animals can hear better than we can? (Dogs, foxes, wolves, horses.) Some can direct their ears towards the sound, others have large ears. What about hares? Bats and dolphins have supersonic hearing. Why is acute hearing useful to them?

Feelings: Children often suppress any negative feelings if they detect any disapproval from adults. If we are concerned by children's attitudes to the natural world, it is essential for them to be open about all feelings, both positive and negative. This is closely related to self-esteem: when children have high self-esteem, they find it easier to express their feelings and thoughts spontaneously and are much less likely to experience pent-up hostility and anger.

Happy, Sad, Angry, Scared: Discuss feelings under these four headings. Talk about when they have felt happy, sad, angry or scared. Let the children draw four pictures to illustrate a time when they have experienced each one.

I Feel: Brainstorm together as many feelings as the children can think of: jealousy, loneliness, anxiety. Ask the children to finish the sentences beginning:

I feel afraid when ....
I feel bored when ....
I feel excited when ....

Faces: Everyone draws a face or makes a paper mask showing an emotion and they are all put into a box. Each child picks out a face or mask and acts out the feeling it shows for the others to guess. Younger children can act out emotions like happy, sad, angry, frightened. Older ones can try to show disappointment, excitement, boredom or surprise, and in pairs they can invent and act out scenarios dealing with these emotions.

Angry Song: "If you're angry and you know it stamp your foot". This is sung to the tune of "If you're happy and you know it". Other emotions and appropriate actions to follow can be improvised. This is a good way of releasing emotions in a secure group situation. (Credit: Linda Williams.)

Feelings Paintings: Which colours do the children think of for different feelings? Red for anger? Or happiness? Pictures can be painted of angry feelings, sad and happy ones.

PEACE AND QUIET

Stillness, Peace and Space: We all need time to ourselves to be quiet and calm - even young children from time to time need tranquillity and space of their own.

Lying on One's Back: One exercise is to get the children to lie down and just shut their eyes for five minutes with no talking. This is best done outside to be more in touch with nature, but if it's wet you can use the school hall.

My Own Space: Let the children move about the room, always keeping to their own space and being careful not to bump into anyone. Then, at a signal, they all crowd into a chalked circle, which is barely large enough to accommodate everyone. What did they feel? Was it too crowded?

VISUALISATION

Human beings have a unique power to imagine they are in a different environment and to visualise images that take them into the world of fantasy. Children, especially, have the ability to enjoy the beauty of the natural world without even leaving the classroom.

Here are some themes that lend themselves to visualisation:

Spaceship: They imagine they are travelling in their own spaceship away from Earth, passing first the moon and then the other planets on to the Milky Way with all of its suns, which we think of as stars. Then they come back to Earth. What did they see? Can they paint a picture of it straight away, with continued silence in the classroom?

My Secret Place: With eyes closed, children could first do simple breathing or relaxation exercises before being led to a secret place, which no one else knows about and which belongs to them alone, and where they will be quite safe. You can improvise a short scenario where they fly out of the classroom, down the stairs, through the doors to the open sky and then land on their very own secret place. They could go on a magic carpet or a beautiful white seagull. Alternatively, the secret place could be made more explicit: a cave or a hollow tree. After quite a long pause, while the children are in their secret place, they could do some creative writing or art work. To keep faith, this follow-up could remain confidential.

Transformations: They have been given the magic power to transform themselves into a creature and they have become birds, flying out of the window over the school, high above the houses, higher still above the town/village, above the ocean and to the warm lands near the equator. They are quite tired and hot so they land on the water's edge and change into fish, swimming in the cool water amongst the coral rocks and beautiful sea anemones. When bigger fish swim by, they hide in a coral cave and so on. Transformations into insects, small rodents, large cats, etc., could follow. This could be taken as a serial activity and should be pleasurable but realistic; when danger or hardship threatens, there could be a speedy transformation. Older children could create their own transformations and lead the class through them.

MY BODY

What do I need to be alive?: Can the children think of all the things they need to be alive? These could be listed on a chart and then illustrated with drawings or collage.

I Need to Breathe: Do some breathing exercises together: taking oxygen in through the nose and breathing out carbon dioxide through the mouth. Children can find out how the lungs work, how they are filled with air and then emptied. Could they demonstrate this using two balloons or paper bags?

The Air we Breathe: Where is air likely to be stuffy? What can we do about it? (See page 54 on air.) If we couldn't breathe what would happen? Stress safety precautions at the swimming baths and the danger of putting a plastic bag over your head.

My Heart Needs to Pump Blood Round my Body: In pairs, can children feel each other's pulse? Some guidance will be needed to locate a spot on the upturned wrist. They should also be able to hear the heart beat by placing their ear on a partner's chest. Older children can time the number of beats in one minute with a stop watch. Do they think that their hearts will beat faster or slower after exercise? They could try skipping, doing high bunny jumps or just walking. Were they right? Can they measure the difference?

I Need to Eat: Make a food diary. How much do they eat in one day? Younger children can illustrate it with pictures and labels, older ones can make fuller records. What makes a balanced diet? They could make a shop with fresh fruit and vegetables, some carbohydrates and protein and encourage "customers" to buy some of each to get the balance right. What does it feel like to be hungry? Could they manage to go without one meal or their mid-morning snack? Children will probably be aware that there are many people in the world who do not have enough to eat.

I Need to Drink: How much do they drink during the day? Can they list what kinds of drinks and how much, for example, a cup of milk. Older children could measure the amount for one day. Does their need to drink vary? Why? Could they manage to go without a drink at playtime? Is it worse to be thirsty or hungry? Children will know about the importance of clean water. (See page 59 on water pollution.) They may also be aware of the problems of people who have to get water from long distances away. How could we save water?

14

I Need Light: What would it be like if there was no sunshine? Could we live without it? Could the plants and animals? Would there be any electricity or gas? (See page 66 on energy from the sun.)

I Need Sleep: Everyone needs a good night's sleep. Find out what time children go to bed and what time they get up. A class bar chart could be made to show the differences. Could the children find out how many hours they sleep? Are the weekend times different? Older children might work out how long they sleep every night and how long they are just resting.

I Need Exercise: How do they exercise their body? Which exercise do they like best? Most sports exercise the body but also use a particular part: eg. football – feet and legs; tennis – hand and arm. Can they think of others? Which kinds of exercise use the whole body? eg. swimming.

The Needs of Animals and Plants: Do animals need the same things as we do? What about plants? Can they think of an animal that they know well and list all of its needs. Can they do the same with a plant? Are there differences? What about breathing?

Body Awareness: Dance lessons can greatly increase children's concepts of all aspects of their bodies. (Reference: Pritchard O & Plant K, The Influence of Dance Teaching on Body Awareness in Primary School Children; £1.50 from the Department of Physical Education, University of Warwick, Coventry CV4 7AL. It includes a teacher's guide with a programme of work.)

Concentration Exercise: A seven-year-old gave me the idea for this exercise. The children have to stand quite still. You call out a part of the body and the children have to exercise that part only, in any way they like. They could take it in turns to call out a body part. Afterwards, they could discuss why they chose the exercise they did.

Full-Length Me: Working in pairs, the children take it in turns to lie on a large sheet of thin cardboard and get a partner to trace round their body; then cut out the silhouette and draw in their face, arms and legs and glue on materials for clothes and hair. These can be used as full-sized puppets for role-play. To help them learn the parts of the body, they could leave the outline on the card and label as many different parts as possible. How can we find out where the heart and lungs are? What is the real shape of the heart?

What do I Measure?: Simple bar charts can be made of the heights and weights of the children in the class. Children will be aware that heights and sizes vary greatly. Discuss the differences, with sensitivity for everyone's feelings. Some unusual measurements they might think of could be the little finger, the length of the foot, round the wrist, round the head.

Comparisons: Ask the children to consider the following: How do I compare in height and weight with my parents? With my teacher? With an elephant? (See page 78 on elephants.) With a blue whale? (See page 81 on whales.)

Caring for my Body: Teeth: It is vital to encourage good dental hygiene from an early age, so when teaching children to care for their bodies, teeth are a good place to start.

Brushing your Teeth: How often do they brush their teeth? How long after eating? Apparently, 40 minutes after eating the rot begins to start! How do they clean them? Get the children to demonstrate. Why do dentists recommend fluoride toothpaste?

A Talk from a Dentist: Many dentists will visit the class to tell children why they need to look after their teeth.

CHAPTER II
SOCIAL
DEVELOPMENT

Co-operation strengthens feelings of success. By working and playing together, children can stimulate each other and begin to have a sense that their power to change things is increased by all of those who join with them. Though they may not express this feeling in words, it will remain as a sense of security which will stand them in good stead in the future.

The principles of co-operation and collaboration underpin many of the activities suggested in this book, so only a few examples are given in this section.

The following two activities could be adapted to whatever theme is being studied, for example if you are doing a topic on "flight", the picture or "film" could be of a bird.

Wall Pictures: Use an overhead projector to enlarge a picture on a wall covered with a large sheet of thin card. Trace the projected image on to the card, then cut it into squares for each child. They can then colour in and reassemble the picture, conferring on which colours to use, or the whole exercise can be a joint effort.

Making a Film: Plan a film together about caring for the planet: for example, making a wildlife garden or a pond, or a documentary style programme about a species under threat. Then if you can get some 16mm clear film from a film laboratory, the children can decide on the sequence of the pictures and share out the drawing and colouring of the animation. To keep this a really simple exercise, the film can have just six frames and be shown through a projector with one of the film makers giving the commentary.

Draw an Animal: In pairs, one child has a drawing or picture of an animal and has to give enough information to his partner for them to be able to draw it. The child with the original drawing or picture must not give the animal's name; his partner should be able to guess what animal he has drawn. If this is too difficult, a sheet of paper can be provided with a general outline in the form of four legs, an oval body and round head and the details can then be added.

CO-OPERATIVE GAMES

There has been a revival of co-operative games in recent years and exciting new ones have been explored. This development has played a substantial role in promoting a non-competitive attitude towards play, where no one is the loser and everyone wins. These activities find a natural progression in environmental education, where children are not only concerned with knowledge of the environment, but also with feelings and attitudes towards it.

Guess the Animal: In groups of three, children choose an animal and decide what to say about it for another team of three to guess. If it isn't guessed, they think of three more things to say about it. Then the other team has a turn. Older children can choose more difficult animals to guess and just take one statement at a time, with the other team following up with another statement about their own animal.

"Who am I?": Divide the class into groups of three. Stick a picture of an animal on to card and attach it to one child's back. The other two in the group, who know what the animal is, answer the questions put

to them about the animal by the cardbearer, but they can only answer "yes", "no" or "perhaps". When the cardbearer has guessed correctly, the others have a turn.

COMMUNICATION

Active Listening: We cannot always listen with complete attention when we are in charge of a large class. Nevertheless, our example when dealing with individuals will pave the way to children's own training in the "art" of active listening.

Listening Games: are favourites with children and a way to get a class quiet! The classic one is to whisper a sentence round the circle and see how it turns out the other end. A winning situation is where it finishes the same, although it may take several attempts to achieve this. This exercise shows how important it is to pay attention to what is said and how easily misunderstandings arise. Choose sentences that are relevant to nature, e.g. "The willow tree whispers in the wind".

Eye to Eye: In pairs, get children to speak to their partner for one minute on a given subject: my favourite game, my pet, my family. They should be sitting parallel, looking straight ahead and not at their partner. They then choose another subject but this time can have eye contact and see all of the body language. Which was the easiest to listen to? What did they feel when their partner did not look them in the face?

PEACEFUL CONFLICT RESOLUTION

Conflictual situations are part of everyday life and systematic methods of dealing with them are being more widely used. The aim is to arrive at a solution which is acceptable to both or all parties - a win-win situation - and it is important for children to learn this approach from an early age. Even quite small children can be shown how to solve their disputes without having recourse to retaliation, whether verbal or physical. They usually need an adult to mediate

for them to begin with, but when they are a little older they can progress to managing the situation on their own. Mediation techniques are now well established in the United States and in many schools there are pupils who are arbitrators, who will give disputants the choice of helping them to settle their conflicts or go to a higher authority. Most children opt for their assistance and this is especially helpful in the playground.

Win-Win: When two children quarrel, they are asked if they would like to negotiate. If they agree, they are told the rule that they must not interrupt when the other has a turn to speak. Then, each one is asked in turn: What happened? How do they feel about it? What would they like ideally to happen? And, finally, what can they agree to as a solution? For example, two children want the same toy car, one snatches it from the other, who promptly hits him, and they are both angry and upset. What each would like is to have a toy all to themselves. Can they think of some realistic solutions, such as to take it in turns, five minutes each; or for one to ride and the other to push or pull him, then change over?

Face to Face: The children face each other in twos in a line. They are given an imaginary conflict situation between two people and they each role-play one of the characters and then, after one minute, change roles and carry on for another minute. The scenarios could be between a teacher and pupil: for example, the child does not want to clear up as she hasn't finished her painting, or between children: one pupil's clay model has been knocked over by someone who shares their table. Younger children can use puppets.

Conflict Situations: Older children could volunteer accounts of their experience of anti-social behaviour: for example, bullying, taking property belonging to others. The class takes one example and two children start to role-play the action. At the moment of conflict they "freeze" and everyone discusses what they think will happen next and the consequences. They brainstorm different ways in which they could resolve the situation and anyone with a proposal can come and act it out, if necessary with a partner. The class discuss the merits of each suggestion and decide on the best solution. Then the original couple act it out. Discussion points could be about the causes leading to the conflict and whether it could have been avoided in the first place.

CHAPTER III
CREATIVE APPROACHES TO THE NATURAL WORLD

CREATIVE STORIES

The following stories, which all have strong connections with the natural world, can be used to stimulate a number of creative approaches or activities. The narrator can stop at a crucial point and ask groups to continue the story themselves, either explaining or acting it to others. They could also interview the characters, asking them how they felt about what was happening and what they would like to happen. Some of the stories could be the inspiration for new versions, perhaps with different characters and situations.

"Giant", J & C Snape: This is the story of a mountain/giant, who is neglected by the villagers. When she goes away the villagers dump all their rubbish in the hole she has left but then nothing will grow there. They beg the mountain to come back and promise never to take her for granted again.

"Mr Grump's Motor Car", J Burningham: Mr Grump takes all the animals for a ride but when the car gets stuck in the mud, the only way out is for everyone to get out and push. The children could have different suggestions for how to get out.

"Oi! Get off our Train", J Burningham: This is the story of a magical train journey where the surprise passengers are animals threatened by hunters, pollution and environmental destruction.

"The Story of Ferdinand", M Leaf: Ferdinand the Bull refuses to fight, preferring his peaceful way of enjoying the sweet flowers of the countryside even in the face of ridicule and pressure. The story offers an example of someone who has the courage of their convictions and could lead to an interesting discussion about peer group pressure. It could also stimulate talk about bullfights and other things that people call sport, like hunting.

"Swimmy", L Lionni: Swimmy is a small fish who persuades all the other small fish to swim closely together in formation so that they appear to be one big fish, and so scare away big fish who might be tempted to eat them. Now they can swim anywhere they like and enjoy all the sights of the ocean without being afraid. What can we do together that one person cannot do so easily?

"The Lorax", Dr Suess: The world in which the Tuffula trees grow is a lovely place until the greedy Onceler chops them all down and builds polluting factories in order to make a new product from the tufts of trees. The Lorax, who observes this happening, deplores the violence to the environment and warns everyone: "Unless..."

"The Swamp Witch", J McCaffrey: Fifinella, the witch, uses so many frogs and insects in her brews that they are in danger of extinction. A mole persuades the witch to start creating potions that help people with their problems and promise never to turn any more creatures into potions, and so the ecological balance of the swamp where they live is restored.

"The Wump World", B Peet: The Wumps, who love their land, are invaded by the Pollutians, who do not care about the environment and are destroying it. What can the Wumps do?

"Sally and the Limpet", S James: Don't mess about with nature is the lesson Sally learns when she gets a limpet stuck on her finger. She manages to find a solution by taking it back to its own habitat. Can the children give other instances where human beings are interfering with nature?

MUSIC

Children enjoy making their own music and their own percussion instruments. They can improvise their own rhythms and the themes they develop are often inspired by nature, whether the rippling of a stream, the roar of the ocean, the sounds of the wind and the rain or the song of the birds.

Refs: "BBC Music Time Pupils' Pamphlet 1990" "BBC The Music Box Song Book", BBC 1987 Desbande, C "Scrape, Rattle and Blow" A & C Black, 1988 Bryt, G "Environmental Songs" The Gould League 1988

Let's Make a Percussion Band: The children make a collection of objects that could be recycled to make a percussion band: large tins, boxes, plastic con-

tainers, cotton reels, rubber bands, rags, pebbles, dowelling, foil and metal bottle tops, jam jars, bottles, strong paper, cardboard, old metal spoons, coat hangers, even an oil drum.

Discuss what different kinds of sounds can be made and what instruments produce them; for example, drums, shakers, rattles, cymbals, castanets, xylophone, zithers, trumpets. In small groups the children discuss and plan which instrument to make.

Ideas could include drums made from containers with greaseproof paper over the top, secured with a rubber band; shakers of varying sized pebbles or sand; cymbals from two tin lids with slots for the hands;

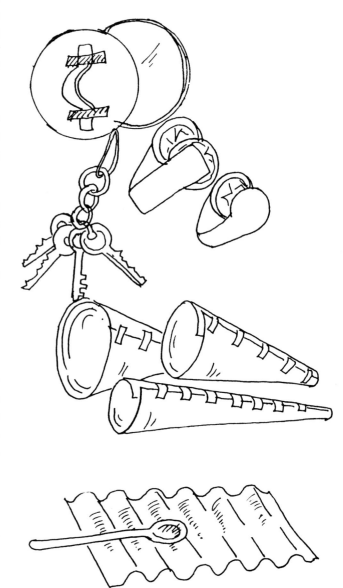

castanets with bottle tops glued to folded card; xylophones using jam jars or bottles filled with different levels of water; rattles out of bottle tops or old keys; zithers with rubber bands of differing thicknesses; trumpets made from rolled-up card. Are the children satisfied with their instruments? Are there ways in which they could change them, for example, using other resources that would have a louder/gentler/sharper sound?

Nature Symphony: Plan a percussion symphony which evokes different aspects of the natural world: the wind in the trees; bird song; the seashore; the ocean waves; a storm starting with distant thunder, rising to a crescendo and then dying away. A script could be read or displayed between the effects. An excerpt from Beethoven's Sixth Symphony could provide inspiration.

Invented Animals: In small groups, children could invent new animals, making a large collage of coloured tissue paper of them and giving them each a name. What sounds or song do they make? What would the sound be like if it was written down? Someone in each group introduces their creature and then the group makes its sound. Why does your creature make this sound? Is it to attract a mate? To keep others away?

Animal Sounds: Make a list of all the animal sounds you can think of. Can you put the animals into groups? For example:

Pets	Domestic animals	Wild animals
Cats mieouw	Sheep baa	Birds sing
Dogs bark	Goats bleat	Frogs croak
Mice squeak	Pigs grunt	Lions roar
Budgies chirp	Horses neigh	Howler monkeys howl

MUSIC AND DRAMA

Peter and the Wolf: Music can be combined with words and actions, as in "Peter and the Wolf" where each character has an instrument and can be acted out. This can be an inspiration for percussion instruments, each one having a sound to represent a creature: animal, bird, reptile or insect. An imaginative story can be invented with characters such as whales, imitated after listening to a tape of whale cries; elephants, with a big drum; butterflies, tinkling on the triangles; snakes, making a rattle sound with seeds in a tin. One idea for a theme is for all the animals under threat to get together and decide that they will all go in a spaceship to another planet! But the humans beg them to stay and promise that they will be taken care of in the future. The experiences that the children have of wildlife should all lend themselves to interpretation through dance and dance-drama.

Animal Dance: The children could improvise a dance which interprets the life-cycle of a particular animal, for example, a butterfly: beginning curled up as an egg, then a caterpillar, finally spinning itself into a cocoon and then gently emerging as a butterfly. Appropriate accompanying music could be the Nutcracker Suite; alternatively, half the class could accompany with percussion music.

DRAMA AND MIME

Drama can bring a heightened awareness of the issues involved in environmental education. It allows the children to explore their own attitudes and values rather than those imposed by the teacher. It can pave the way towards a consideration of other points of view, including those of the rest of the creatures and plants on this earth, and it is also the key to an understanding of the more abstract concepts concerned with the threat to the planet.

Making Masks: Masks are an inspiration for improvised drama and role play and are often sufficient to portray the role that is being played. Simple ones can be made from paper plates or cut-out cardboard with elastic thread through the back. Many animals lend themselves to full face masks; for example, the cat family, primates and owls, whereas side faces can be cut out double and stapled at the top for wolves, foxes and dogs. Often masks cover half the face with large openings for eyes and fitting over the nose, leaving the nostrils and mouth free; otherwise large

openings have to be cut for eyes, nose and mouth in the circular ones. More ambitious masks are made by modelling them in clay, greasing them on the outside and covering them with papier mache which is removed when dry. All kinds of masks can be painted and adorned with hair.

Animal Points of View: Working in pairs wearing masks, children imagine they are two animals holding a conversation. For example, a hen could talk to a fox. Other ideas could be a rose, a greenfly and a ladybird; or a spider, a web and a fly.

Threatened Homes Role-play: Older children could talk about animals whose homes are being threatened with destruction by human activity; for example, hedges are being cut down to make way for larger fields; new motorways are cutting through the countryside; a big housing estate is being built near a village; the village duck pond is being drained. Further afield, the trees in the rain forests are being logged.

In planning a role-play, they should try to put themselves in the animal's place. They have to think of leaving their home. Where will they go? Will they be safe on their journey? Would they be shot, or run over? Would they have enough to eat? What about their babies? They can decide on a very simple scenario, perhaps a meeting of all the threatened animals to decide what to do. Having chosen the habitat that is threatened, they could list the animals that would be involved. Some might decide to leave immediately, others to stay and try to adapt; some might suggest appealing to humans, as they are the cause of the disruption. This might lead to a scene where the animals appeal to some children playing nearby. The children want to keep the hedges, the duck pond or the common where they play and so they agree to ask the adults to stop the development. If it can't be stopped, what can be done? (Could a wildlife area be built nearby?)

To help the children develop greater empathy towards the animal characters, they could first act out scenes from such classics as "The Wind in the Willows" "Tarka the Otter" and "Chantecleer" or any of the story books listed on pages 19–20.

PUPPETS

Puppets help children to express themselves more freely and overcome their shyness. They are an especially good media for enacting themes relating to the care of the environment, ranging from the problems of litter to the predicament of animals under threat. There are numerous kinds of puppets, all of which children can make themselves, albeit in a simplified form.

What Kinds of Puppets?: The children can brainstorm and list different kinds of puppets: glove, hand, finger, cut-out, string, stick, shadow. They can suggest a range of resources to explore various models: cloth, wood, clay, paper, paint, dolls and toy animals, string, thread, glue, sellotape, paper clips.

These resources can be assembled and displayed in categories and, in small groups, the children can experiment with designing and making their own puppets. One group might try different ways of making **glove puppets** with paper bags, old mittens, cut-out patterns, old socks; another could explore **finger puppets** - knitted, cardboard cylinders, cut-outs on rings, tips of old gloves, **shadow puppets** - cardboard shapes with sticks; **string puppets** - articulated with round paper clips; **full-length puppets** cut out in card round their bodies; stick puppets with heads of hollowed Plasticine or as a base for papier mache. Younger children are best with a limited choice at any one time: glove or finger puppets are good to begin with.

Puppet Scenarios: These can be spontaneous with a lot of ad-libbing. A good introduction to this kind of drama is to practise with bare hands, which can be very expressive, and mimed with a "voice-over". Hand puppets can be successful as shadows on a screen or wall, especially when the dialogue is between two different animals. The stories of Aesop and La Fontaine are a good source of inspiration for puppet scenarios and present value systems in an acceptable way.

Recycling Scenario: One by one the puppets throw something into the dustbin and each time another puppet stops them in time and tells them how it could be recycled.

Litter: The children go for a picnic near a river or the sea and throw their litter in and near the water: banana skins, crisp packets, plastic bags and bottles. The creatures living there rise out of the water and tell the children to take all their rubbish home with them. A frog has had a sweet wrapper caught in its throat in mistake for a damsel fly; a fish has got its fins caught in the remains of a fishing net. The puppeteers have to decide on the venue: river, sea or pond, and choose appropriate creatures, all of whom could protest about their habitat being cluttered with rubbish.

Glove Puppet Theatre: A puppet theatre can be made using an open cardboard box on its side with the bottom cut out and a curtain taking its place at the bottom. If it is placed on a desk, draped with an old curtain down to the ground, the legs of the puppeteers will not be seen and they can put their glove puppets under the theatre curtain to act.

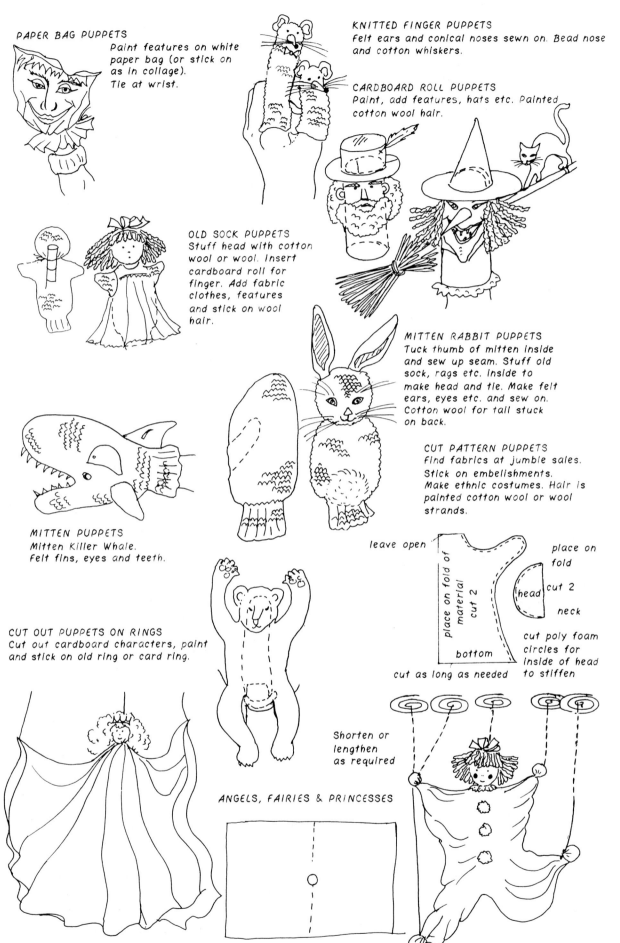

PAPER BAG PUPPETS
Paint features on white paper bag (or stick on as in collage). Tie at wrist.

KNITTED FINGER PUPPETS
Felt ears and conical noses sewn on. Bead nose and cotton whiskers.

CARDBOARD ROLL PUPPETS
Paint, add features, hats etc. Painted cotton wool hair.

OLD SOCK PUPPETS
Stuff head with cotton wool or wool. Insert cardboard roll for finger. Add fabric clothes, features and stick on wool hair.

MITTEN RABBIT PUPPETS
Tuck thumb of mitten inside and sew up seam. Stuff old sock, rags etc. inside to make head and tie. Make felt ears, eyes etc. and sew on. Cotton wool for tail stuck on back.

CUT PATTERN PUPPETS
Find fabrics at jumble sales. Stick on embellishments. Make ethnic costumes. Hair is painted cotton wool or wool strands.

MITTEN PUPPETS
Mitten Killer Whale. Felt fins, eyes and teeth.

CUT OUT PUPPETS ON RINGS
Cut out cardboard characters, paint and stick on old ring or card ring.

leave open

place on fold of material cut 2

place on fold

cut 2

head

neck

bottom

cut as long as needed

cut poly foam circles for inside of head to stiffen

Shorten or lengthen as required

ANGELS, FAIRIES & PRINCESSES

White silk or muslin rectangle. Head stuffed with wool and tied hair made with wool fleece. Nose, eyes and mouth painted on. Gold paper crown. Attach cotton thread to head and silk arms and feet.

Shadow Puppet Theatre: A simple structure can be made by putting two pieces of cane 50 cms long into separate plant pots filled with heavy earth. Place them about 100 cms apart and glue or tape tracing paper (from a drawing office supply shop) between them to form a screen, which is put on a table. In a darkened room, shine a lamp on the back of the screen and hold the puppets near the screen, against the light, throwing their shadows on to the screen.

ART

Art plays a great part in helping us to visualise and recreate the wonders of the natural world - drawings, paintings, collages, murals, modelling, printing, sculpture and constructing - and almost all of the activities in this book can be illustrated in some of these forms.

The skills of direct observation are intrinsically linked to the interpretation of the environment and they can be expressed through a whole variety of artistic media.

Drawing and Painting: Young children will sketch and paint quite spontaneously whatever they have experienced at first hand. Collaborative painting of murals can depict subjects varying from traffic jams and factories to regions such as the rainforests or the desert.

Clay Modelling: Clay is ideal for making models of animals children have seen while on visits to city or rural farms. Self-hardening clay takes about two to three days to harden and during that time it can be worked on; it can be kept soft longer by covering it with polythene.

Sand Painting: This is a visual and tactile approach which can be used to depict mountains, deserts, lakes or roads, and in appropriate colours: the sea, the sky, forests and trees. The technique is quite simple: mix silver sand with powder paint and sprinkle on areas that have been painted with paste.

Group Sculpture: Give each child a ball of clay or playdough the size of an orange and ask them to make any shape they like, but they must use up all of their clay. Place a large sheet of coloured cardboard in the centre of the room and let the children add their contribution, one at a time to the group sculpture. Let them view it from all sides and discuss how they feel about it. Alternatively, they can decide on a theme beforehand, such as a pond, garden, landscape, farm, zoo, village or park.

Plaster Sculpture: Older children can make plaster by adding double the amount of plaster to water to make a paste like thick cream. Pour it into yogurt containers, lined with clingfilm, stir it and leave to harden. It can then be taken out and carved with a modelling tool into an animal. Another carving medium is a bar of kitchen soap. Children could learn about the Inuits who still carve out of soapstone. (Reference "An Arctic Child" Lyle, S and Roberts, M, Greenlight Publications, 1988.)

PRINTING

Vegetable Printing: Besides making the traditional patterns with vegetable prints cut horizontally, they can be cut vertically and printed in the correct colours to illustrate a gardening catalogue, a greengrocer's shop or collage of a kitchen garden.

Junk Printing: How many articles can be used for printing? Cotton reels, cardboard cylinders, lids, boxes, string, corks. The prints could make a backdrop for a puppet play on junk or a poster on litter.

Batik and Tie Dye: These processes, which originated in Africa and the East, can help children to appreciate the expression of colour and pattern which is a feature of the art of so many self-sufficient communities. The finished lengths of material can be used for drama or made into hangings.

27

Young children can begin with paper: they first paint a wash over the whole surface, then use a wax crayon or candle to make a design, and then wash over with another colour, and so on. This gives them experience in mixing colours. Can they guess what will happen when the first wash is yellow, for example, and the second one is blue?

Traditional batik has a similar process, but instead of candles or crayons, melted wax is painted on cotton and then dyed in cold water. Safety note: This is only suitable for older children under careful supervision. Tie dye is similar: it uses knots and string twisted round parts of the cotton cloth to resist the dye. Plain cotton handkerchiefs can be given a new lease of life by this method, or mats and cushion covers can be made.

Costumes for Drama: (Reference: Oxfam, Alaro: An activity pack about resist dyed cloths, using different printing techniques, with children making their own designs, using plants and lichens for experimenting)

WEAVING

When children understand the basic principles of weft and warp, they can experiment with their own ideas on different ways of weaving. They can progress from table mats woven with coloured sticky paper to simple looms made out of old shoe boxes, threading wool through holes to make the warp and using a cardboard shuttle for the weft. They should use their inventive powers to design and make their own looms. Their first-hand experience will help them to relate to peoples who have a long tradition of hand-weaving, for example, the American Indians.

Woven Hangings: The warp can be knotted round a slat of wood at the top and another, which is weighted with clay, at the bottom. The weft can be in the form of natural objects such as ivy, bark, mosses and twigs, taken from the ground. Can the children work out how to save themselves the trouble of going in and out between each thread? Instead of natural items, they could weave strips of brightly coloured material.

Recycling Paper: Making paper is well worth the effort as it gives children a real experience of recycling. You need a food processor to pulp the paper in water or alternatively, tear it up by hand in to minute pieces and soak it. A small frame with nylon mesh stapled on to it can be made out of old wooden picture frames, otherwise four pieces of wood can be screwed together.

Soak the pulped paper in a baking dish and then dip the frame right underneath so that pulp is spread out on the nylon side as evenly as possible. Shake it a little and turn it upside down. The paper should cling to the mesh. Place it on a wet piece of blanket. Squeeze out the water by drawing your hand over the top of the mesh and the paper will be spread out on the blanket. You can repeat the process putting a kitchen cloth between the first paper and the next, and so on. If the children want coloured paper, they can colour the water with powder paint or permanent ink. They can make a multi-coloured effect by placing various colours in different parts of the tray. The paper can be trimmed and made into greeting cards with "handmade paper by..." on them. Note: Newspaper turns out grey unless it is first bleached in the sun with vinegar. Never use bleach for recycling paper as it causes poisonous waste. (Reference: Paper, Tidy Britain Group).

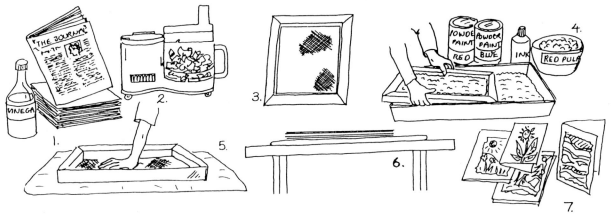

PHOTOGRAPHY

Children's knowledge of the wider world of nature is built up by a series of visual images, which they need to assimilate and relate to their own lives. Children can be quite expert at using simple cameras and this gives full play to their imagination and their own choices.

The Changing Classroom: Each child has a chance to photograph some part of the classroom over a period of time. The results can be put in a sequence, showing the changes in display, the clothes children are wearing, the weather, etc. Can they stand exactly where the photographer was and see if there are any further differences? Discuss the reasons for the changes.

A Walk round the School Grounds: A series of photos can be taken to show various aspects such as wild flower areas, a pond, favourite trees and plants in tubs. These can be mounted with a description of how these areas were cultivated and what is in them. If your grounds are limited to a concrete playground, then arrange a walk to the park. Books of labelled photographs can record seasonal changes. Sequencing these snaps is a good introduction to story writing with captions or speech bubbles. This process can be used effectively to illustrate systematically how something was grown, like sunflowers; or planned and created, like a pond or a wildlife area.

Framing: Brainstorm all the different things we can look through to make a frame. Apart from the camera viewfinder, there are windows, and all sorts of cut-outs in cardboard that the children can make themselves: circles, rectangles, ovals. There are also cardboard tubes, magnifying glasses and empty picture frames. This exercise enables children to appreciate the choices that can be made about what to include and what will remain outside the picture. They can also use their hands cupped together as viewfinders.

Collecting Photographs: Children can be given a theme and then collect and cut out any photos they can find in magazines. The theme can be any area that is dealt with in this book: pets, parks, farms, threatened species, or "families like mine." With the family theme it is interesting to get them to look at possible stereotypes. They can cut out the characters in the pictures and put them in different situations: Dads at the cooker, Mums driving a bus! Photopacks with ideas on these approaches are: "What is a family?" "Working Now" "Behind the Scenes" and "Doing things in and about the house." They explore all sorts of activities with usual and unusual images depicted by photographs. (Reference: Birmingham Development Education Centre.)

Photo Questions: In small groups, children ask as many questions as they can think of about certain photographs, for example, "What does the photographer want to tell us?" "What has the photographer left out?" "Can you draw in what would be included if the picture was extended?".

Making a Mini-Cartoon: Get the children to draw a series of actions on a notepad, one on each page, starting at the back. An example of a sequence is illustrated. Then flick through the pictures from back to front to see, for example, plants growing and dying, a squirrel eating nuts, a chicken coming out of an egg. If the paper is fairly thin, they can see a faint outline on the previous page to trace, making the slight change needed to show the motion. This is a first step to knowing how films are made.

COLLECTING AND CLASSIFICATION

Children are natural classifiers: they have an in-built capacity to order their world, classifying their concepts by means of experiences and language. In the same way, nature can be classified in families. Trees can be put into categories of deciduous and evergreen; flowers can be linked by their families. Animals can be divided broadly into mammals and egg-laying creatures.

Children can be encouraged to plan their own classifications: plants that are either cultivated or wild; animals that are domestic or wild. Further divisions can be explored: plants that are either grown for their seeds (wheat), for their leaves (lettuce), for their roots (carrots) or for their flowers (roses).

A Collecting Expedition: Children can go in small groups to collect a variety of objects in the school grounds, an area of common land or, where feasible, the seashore. They will need to wear plastic gloves. It is important to discuss with children beforehand what sort of things they can collect and what must be left undisturbed.

On their return to the classroom they can review and discuss their findings. How can they sort them out and put them into categories of similarity? It is good for them to handle the objects and try out different ways of dividing them. They might put stones and

pebbles together and all the things that are parts of plants in another group. Can they divide them again? Into leaves, twigs, seeds? Could the leaves be divided again? For example, into brown and green?

They will have found quite a lot of litter: bottle tops, bottles, tins, paper, lolly sticks, etc. How can they be classified? Metal, glass, paper, plastic? Or they could sort them into various types of containers: bottles, plastic bags, cartons, crisp packets.

The containers could be sub-divided again: transparent, brown and green bottles, round or square cartons. They need to decide which categories to choose. Can they divide all of the objects into two main groups? Growing things and minerals? Manmade and natural? If the latter is chosen, each child should choose one object and in turn put it in the appropriate group.

Now we can ask for a volunteer or a small group to sort out the natural objects into sub- groups, for example, stones, leaves, seeds, or growing things and inanimate. Similarly, with the man-made pile, subgroups could be designated. The result should be a pyramid of objects on the floor or a large table.

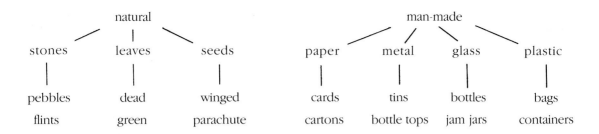

Older children could continue to sub-divide, for example into aluminium and stainless steel in the metal section.

Their classifications can be recorded individually or on a large chart, with labels and drawings. Alternatively, the children can concentrate on litter only and this will be a basis for their activities in dealing with it on a wider scale as whole school or community action.

Collections: Children can be encouraged to make their own collections: shells from the seashore can be grouped according to whether they are bi-valved or single, also by size and shape; stamps depicting

animals or flowers could be sorted according to whether they are threatened or not.

Recycling Resources: Most schools have a number of boxes in the resource cupboard where all sorts of materials and objects can be used for creative activities and construction. As above, get the children to sort them: for example, a paper box, a container box, a fabric box and an odds and ends box. How does it help to have the items sorted and labelled?

By choosing how to group their objects, children will learn that there are many different ways of classification according to the categories that they themselves establish.

CHAPTER IV

THE SCHOOL AND NATURE

A Whole School Approach: Many schools now adopt an integrated approach to environmental education and have a policy which sets out the ways in which it can be incorporated into the National Curriculum on a cross-curricular basis. They create opportunities for children to explore and understand the world of nature through classroom activities as well as organising visits to parks, nature centres and the countryside as part of their school's programme of work on the environment. In this way, children develop a respect for their school and its grounds, and the environmental needs of the local community.

Experiences with Nature: Children have a natural inclination to care for living things, particularly animals, and teachers and parents can do much to foster and extend this. Their daily experiences will help to promote respect for the living world, for example, learning to leave flowers to grow in their natural surroundings. They can usually pick up plenty of leaves from the ground for their studies, and green twigs should only be picked for a particular reason, taking care not to spoil the shape of the bush or tree.

Similarly, contact with animals will promote an understanding of their needs and their place in the order of things. Many creatures that have invoked fear or disgust will be accepted as living beings in their own right.

The ideal way to appreciate nature is to experience it "in the wild" although there are many activities that can take place in the classroom, especially growing things, enabling children to appreciate the cyclic nature of all growth and the similarities between the needs of plants and animals and those of ourselves. The study of animals is best done in their habitat, but it is possible to take smaller creatures back to the classroom for a few days in order to observe them more closely, understand their needs, and learn how to care for them.

In all of these activities there will be note-taking and sketching; children could make their own note and sketch books from stiff cardboard and sheets of paper stapled together with a pencil attached. There should also be much sorting and classifying, setting up of simple experiments, recording results and attempts to explain and evaluate findings.

PLANTS

Growing Plants: Growing from carrot, parsnip and turnip tops and potato eyes are familiar favourites; likewise pips and stones, for example, avocados, oranges, lemons and apples. Why not sprout food that is nutritious and full of protein, such as aduki and mung beans, chick peas and lentils? They need to be soaked overnight and rinsed twice daily for two to five days, when they can be eaten in salads or sandwiches. Although sprouting kits can be bought, the children could devise their own. Polystyrene trays can be pierced with holes or simply line a plastic container with cotton wool to grow mustard and cress. Growing food will encourage children to taste new flavours and lead them towards a more nutritious diet.

All the experiments in growth can be drawn or photographed at regular intervals and labelled. Older children should keep records of exactly what they did. If there are failures, encourage them to think about what went wrong. Did the plants dry out? Were the sprouts bitter if they were left too long before eating?

The following questions should prompt some valuable investigations: What do we need in order to grow? Food, drink, light, space, exercise. Which of these do the plants need? Is growing their exercise? How can you show that plants need food? What could we grow them in? Cotton wool, compost, gravel, clay, nothing at all? Which do you think would grow best? Which worst? Supposing you gave them extra nourishment: seaweed solution, grass cuttings, ash, organic fertiliser? What would you have to do to make sure the results are fair? (Use the same number of seeds, the same sized containers, the same amounts of the material they are grown in.) Some plants grow

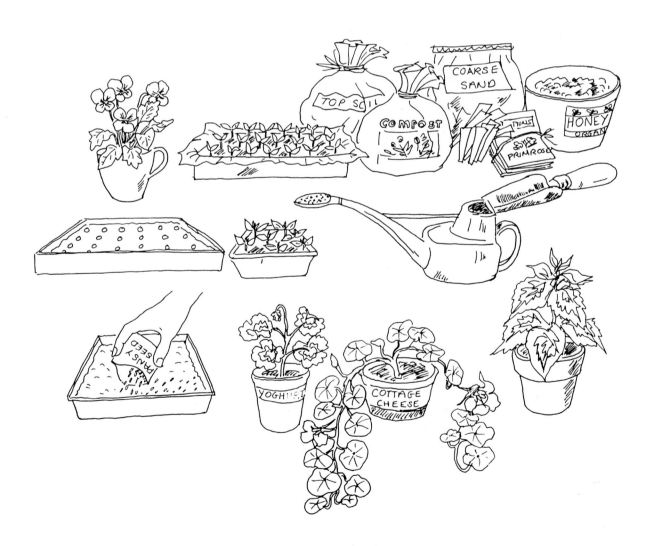

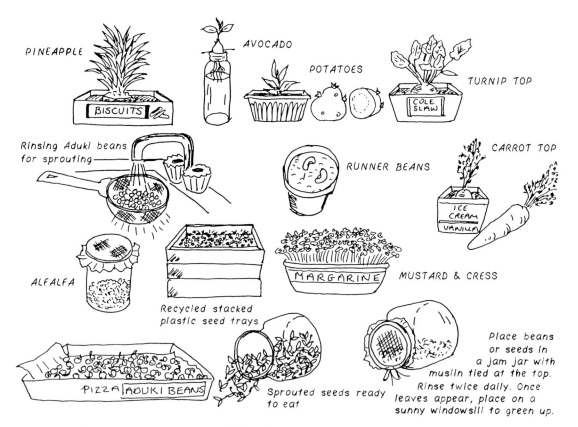

PINEAPPLE

BISCUITS

AVOCADO

POTATOES

TURNIP TOP

COLE SLAW

Rinsing Aduki beans for sprouting

RUNNER BEANS

CARROT TOP

ICE CREAM VANILLA

ALFALFA

Recycled stacked plastic seed trays

MARGARINE

MUSTARD & CRESS

PIZZA ADUKI BEANS

Sprouted seeds ready to eat

Place beans or seeds in a jam jar with muslin tied at the top. Rinse twice daily. Once leaves appear, place on a sunny windowsill to green up.

best in poor soil; try nasturtiums in gravel, half sand and half earth and in oil and see which has the best flowers.

Do the plants need light? What happens if they are put in the dark? Then in the light? What colour are the shoots? Why? See if they have produced roots.

Experiment with water. What happens if you give too much water, or too little? Why do you think some plants need more water than others? What sort of plants need very little water? Which need a lot? Cacti store water in their leaves - why? Encourage children to be careful in their experiments in watering and rescue their plants in time, so that they don't die.

Plants like enough space to grow. Can children make an experiment to show this? What differences do they notice between the ones that have plenty of space and the ones that are crowded? Plants also need warmth. How could they show that? Some plants - perennials - live outside throughout the winter; others, called annuals, have to be planted each spring. What about plants from hot countries, like African violets? Could they survive our winters?

Plant Problems: Does a plant know which way to grow? (Roots downwards, shoots upwards?) The children could plant four large beans in different positions against blotting paper in a transparent container, with water at the bottom, then observe and record what happens. How does the water reach

the bean? If a plant bends over towards the light, how can they make it straight? (By propping it up? Turning it?) Can they think of other ways to show how plants must grow towards the light? (Plant them in a closed cardboard box with an opening at the far end.) Do they do the same in search of water? How could the children find out? Supposing there were obstacles in the way, would the plant overcome them? See if the children can devise a test to find out.

Taking Cuttings: New plants can be made by taking a cutting just under the joint, stripping off the lower leaves and planting it in a suitable mixture (see "Growing from Seed" below). Choose a cutting that has not flowered and, if possible, dip it in hormone rooting powder. If you keep the cutting in water you can see the roots forming before you plant it in the soil. Geraniums and busy lizzies respond well to this treatment.

Plants from Leaves: Just remove a lower leaf of an African violet and put it in a pot with some good compost. (African violets can also be divided, when they form rosettes, to make new plants.) African violets are now virtually extinct in the wild, as they have become such a popular pot plant all over the world.

Changing Plants: Challenge children to find examples of different stages in a plant's life, from seeds, buds and young sprouts to full grown and then to decayed and dead ones. Can they find any damaged plants? What do they think caused the damage? They could make a chart of the cycle of plant life.

SEEDS

Observing Seeds: Children can observe seeds under a magnifying glass and note their similarities and differences. Why are they shaped differently?

WINGED DISPERSAL

Sycamore

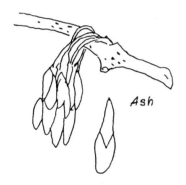

Ash

EXPLOSIVE DISPERSAL

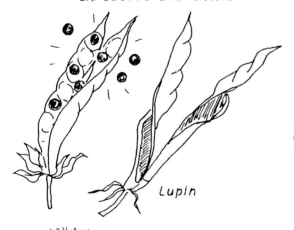

Lupin

WIND DISPERSAL

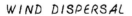

Dandelion

Poppy

Collecting Seeds: In autumn, a great variety of seeds can be collected, classified and mounted. Guidelines for approaches to classification are on page 35. They could be divided into methods of dispersal: airborne (dandelion), explosive (violet), by birds (holly), clinging to animals (burdock), etc. Younger children could concentrate on airborne seeds, such as thistles, dandelions, old man's beard, sycamore and ash. They could drop them from a height and observe what they do. If they simulate wind with a hair dryer (NB safety!), they can see what happens to these seeds when the wind blows.

Growing from Seed: Children can weigh out a potting mixture of equal amounts of coarse sand (for drainage), top soil (for bacteria and fungi), and compost (for food). Would it be the same if they filled a container with each material? How could they find out the differences? (Weigh the volumes and compare them with the actual weights.) They can grow all sorts of vegetables, herbs and flowers: radishes, carrots, lettuce, and even potatoes, rosemary, and annuals like marigolds, tobacco plants and basil. Dampen the soil and plant the seeds sparsely, covering them with a little more mixture, and put a plastic bag over them until they sprout. Many of these plants can be enjoyed by the children as snacks.

Dried Herbs: Herbs can also be dried and made into presents such as herb sachets or pillows. Bags of dried rosemary and mint can protect clothes against moths, without using chemicals.

ANIMAL DISPERSAL

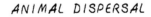

Blackberry

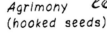

Agrimony
(hooked seeds)

Lime

Use your own Seeds: Collect the seeds when the flowers have dried and store them in an envelope, keeping them in a cool place until it is time to plant them. This is much more economical than buying packets of seeds. How much money can they save each time they use their own seeds?

Seeds are Everywhere: What happens when they dig up a clod of earth and put it in a shallow container on a sunny windowsill, watering it frequently? What seeds have been hiding there? They can even do the same with some dust from walls or paved areas; some little plants will probably emerge.

PLANT DISTRIBUTION

Ask children first how they would set about finding out the plant distribution in a given area. Younger ones could be given one of these four examples. Older pupils might be able to think of other ways.

Plant 'Hoopla': There are many ways of finding out what plants grow in a certain area: a common one is to put a PE hoop on an area where there is a good variety of wildlife and see how many different plants can be seen in the circle. Which are the most common? Which are the most rare?

Stringing Along: Another idea is to have a long piece of string, tied to a stake at both ends so that it passes through a selection of plant life. How many different kinds of plants does the string touch. Can they draw a plan showing them?

Giant Strides: Children enjoy this activity. They must take a certain number of steps, say four, and at each step see how many different objects they can touch. They then re-trace their steps and see if they can remember everything. A partner can help to check.

See-through Circles: Cut out large circles of transparent plastic and peg them into the ground where there is a wide variety of plants. Using felt pens, the children mark out any plants they can see below. In the classroom, children can compare notes and see which ones they have in common. They can make simple charts with sketches of the plants that are most common, putting ticks or numbers to show how many there were.

TREES

Tree Areas: Trees are a great source of wonder: how can a tiny acorn or beech nut produce such a miracle? Trees give us wood and provide habitats for countless creatures. But with forests being destroyed at a colossal rate, it is becoming particularly important for children to know of their immense value. If children try to grow their own trees from seed, they will appreciate just how long a tree takes to grow.

My Own Tree: It is good if children can adopt their own special tree, preferably in the school grounds or in a nearby park, which can be visited regularly. They can make a book of drawings of their tree at different seasons of the year, illustrating its leaves, flowers and seeds and making rubbings of its bark.

How Old is My Tree?: First, they need to find out the girth of the tree in centimetres or inches. This can be done in pairs with each child's tree being measured in turn. A rough estimate is that if a tree is in a wood, $1\frac{1}{4}$ centimetres or $\frac{1}{2}$ inch equal one year; if it is in the open, $2\frac{1}{2}$ centimetres or 1 inch represent a year. Does a tree grow more quickly in a wood or in the open? Why is this?

How Tall is My Tree?: Take a photograph of the child next to their adopted tree. How many times taller is the tree? Measure the child and then multiply the height by the number of times the tree is taller in the photograph.

A Tree through the Seasons: Discuss all the changes that can take place with the inhabitants in or near a particular tree during the year. It needs to be a tree that they can visit. What creatures live in or near it? Squirrels, owls, rabbits, moles, field mice, woodpeckers and various birds including the migrating cuckoo? To find out what insects live in the tree, put a white sheet or an umbrella on the ground beneath and shake a bough above it. The insects can be examined on the spot with a magnifying glass; put them in a glass jar with a paint brush and return them to the tree afterwards. To catch ground insects, a trap can be made by putting a jam jar in the ground and covering it with a tile propped up by small stones. How can mini-beasts be attracted to it? (Put a little piece of fruit or meat in the jar.)

In pairs, children choose a creature and find out about it from books in the school library; non-readers can find out quite a lot from labelled picture books. Then each pair prepares a sentence or two that their animal might say for each season; they write it down or dictate it into a tape recorder. This project needs to be started in the autumn term and continued throughout the school year. By the end of the summer term, they could listen to the whole tape and discuss what they might have added.

LEAVES AND FLOWERS

Leaves and Flowers from Buds: In late winter, take some small twigs from trees in the school grounds and put them in water. The buds will open in the warm atmosphere of the classroom and the leaves will gradually unfold. The children could take photographs of the different stages or draw them as a sequence. To note the changes in growth, they could tie on coloured wool or mark them with a felt pen. The horse chestnut with its sticky buds and bunches of pink or white flowers is a favourite; also early flowering shrubs like forsythia will bloom with their bright yellow flowers.

Leaf Changes: Pick up autumn leaves from one particular tree and make a sequence from leaves that are still green, through all the ranges of colour, to the final rusty brown of a dead leaf or a skeleton.

They could be pasted in order in a book of autumn leaves, one page for each tree.

Matching Plants: Each child is given a picture of a flower, leaf or grass and they have to see if they can find it growing in the wild. These need to be chosen amongst plants that are in the immediate vicinity: the school grounds or a safe park. They can make a joint collage with their collections.

Rain on Leaves: Ask children to collect a number of different leaves - shiny, matt, hairy, spiky - and sort them according to their feel (their texture). Then, with a watering can (with a rose if outside, or with a spray), sprinkle some water on them. Which ones get rid of the water quickest? What happens with the hairy ones?

Leaf Rubbing: Place a leaf face down on a sheet of card and put a piece of paper over it. Then rub it evenly with a wax crayon and the impression of the leaf and its tracery of veins will come through. It is best to use strong leaves with well defined veins for this exercise.

ANIMALS IN THE CLASSROOM

Studying Creatures: Whenever possible, animals should be studied in their natural environment, where they can be sketched and observed in action. (Some can be caught and examined on the spot.) If it is necessary to observe them in the classroom over a period of days, their habitat should be "recreated" as far as possible, and the creatures released to the place from where they were taken. Many children have developed an aversion to some "mini-beasts" and by taking an active interest in them, their feelings can often be overcome. An understanding of how such creatures function enables children to realise how they play an essential part in the whole scheme of things, and how many species are threatened by human activity. The children should keep simple records and drawings of the creatures they have studied and show their differences and similarities.

Butterflies: Butterflies can be observed while they are feeding from their favourite flowers, like the buddleia. What can the children find out about them? How many legs do they have? How many body sections? The children could make a sketch of them resting and in flight. What is the difference?

CATERPILLAR HOUSE

fix muslin over neck of container with a rubber band.

Clear plastic container with bottom cut off and lid discarded. Press firmly into soil.

favourite food plant of caterpillars replaced each day.

Cotton wool at neck to stop caterpillars falling into the water.

Small jar with water.

Cardboard ramp for easy access to plant food.

Container filled with damp soil.

Butterfly Paintings: Fold a piece of thin card in half and open it out. Then paint half a colourful butterfly with its body on the fold line. Fold again while the paint is wet and press hard to make a symmetrical image. If possible, base the paintings on sketches of real specimens and name them. They can be left as a mounted painting or cut out and fastened to twigs of greenery, keeping their wings upright. A mobile could also be made from the artwork. The same process can be carried out for moths, and dragon or damsel flies. Alternatively, they could be modelled with pipe cleaners as the body and wings made out of tissue paper glued to thin wire frames.

Keeping Caterpillars: Although you cannot keep butterflies in the classroom, you can of course keep caterpillars which will spin a cocoon and later emerge as butterflies, which should then be released immediately near the sort of flowers they like. Can the children think of all the caterpillar's needs - food, water, safety; can they supply them all? See if they can design a home for their caterpillar. One idea is given here. Is it like theirs? Let them watch the caterpillar eating. How many leaves does it eat every day, or does it eat parts of leaves? What would happen if they forgot to put the plant it feeds on into water?

Stick Insects: These perfect examples of camouflage can be treated similarly to caterpillars. They need plenty of fresh privet. Children can make a drawing and challenge friends to find the stick insect. This can initiate a discussion on camouflage in other animals and why they are hidden in this way. Is it always to escape their predators?

Ladybirds: These are great favourites and can be examined easily under containers with magnifying tops. Can the children find different kinds of ladybirds? How many spots do they have? What colours? Why are they so popular with gardeners? Why are they not camouflaged? A chart could be made comparing ladybirds with butterflies: See opposite.

This kind of wall chart can be extended to compare any creatures studied and children could include the number of legs and body segments, etc. For example, spiders have eight legs and insects six, spiders two body sections, insects three.

Bees: Children can watch bees going from one flower to another. Can they see what happens? How do the bees get the nectar? What does the plant get in return? How does the pollen stick on the bee's back? Questions such as these will come spontaneously from the children. Quite a few people keep bees, even in town gardens. A friendly bee keeper could answer all the questions: for example, how do bees tell others where they have found a wealth of flowers with nectar?

Honey Tasting: A honey-tasting session would be a special treat with different flower flavours, if possible, including local honey, which could be compared with imported brands.

Homes for Small Bees: Small bees like to live in tiny cylinders that are brightly coloured. What can the children suggest? Where should they put the new homes?

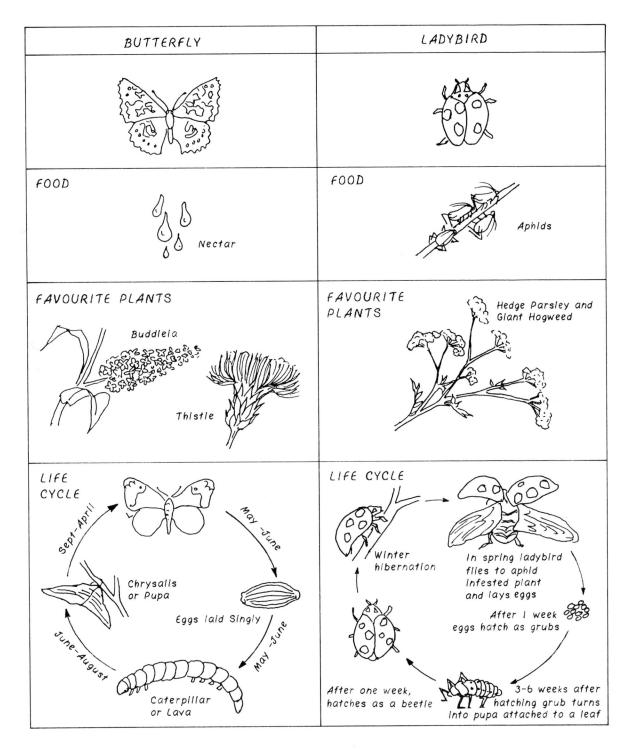

BUTTERFLY	LADYBIRD
FOOD	FOOD
Nectar	Aphids
FAVOURITE PLANTS	FAVOURITE PLANTS
Buddleia	Hedge Parsley and Giant Hogweed
Thistle	
LIFE CYCLE	LIFE CYCLE
Sept-April	Winter hibernation
May-June	In spring ladybird flies to aphid infested plant and lays eggs
Chrysalis or Pupa	After 1 week eggs hatch as grubs
Eggs laid Singly	
June-August	May-June
Caterpillar or Lava	After one week, hatches as a beetle
	3-6 weeks after hatching grub turns into pupa attached to a leaf

Which Colours do Bees Prefer?: Put little dabs of honey on different coloured cards and make a note of the number of visits bees make to each one. Do they prefer dark brown or black? Older children can make a graph of this.

Growing Borage: Borage has often been called bee borage because bees find it so attractive. Grow it in a container or a window box.

Making an Insect Garden: This can even be managed in a concrete playground if no other green space is available, although it is better near a small pond area, which attracts many insects. Many of the plants that attract insects can be grown in pots, containers or "gro-bags". Start with ones that you know attract insects, such as buddleia, thistles, giant hogweed, nettles (from seed); then choose sweet smelling ones like wallflowers, sweet william and lavender. Each group might have a tub and find out from books and catalogues how to stock it. Your own seed will save expense. Remember to put some old logs and stones nearby for tiny insects to hide. Each group can list and label what they have planted on a seasonal basis.

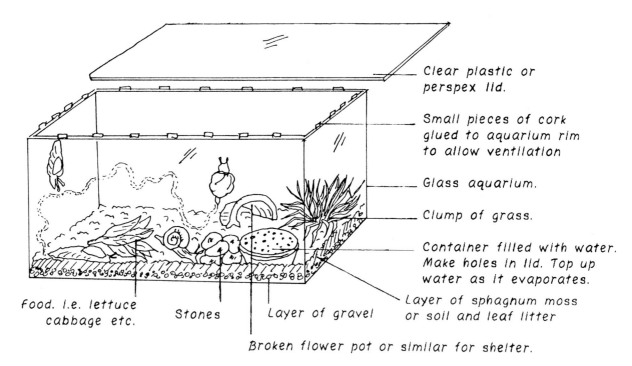

Clear plastic or perspex lid.

Small pieces of cork glued to aquarium rim to allow ventilation

Glass aquarium.

Clump of grass.

Container filled with water. Make holes in lid. Top up water as it evaporates.

Layer of sphagnum moss or soil and leaf litter

food. i.e. lettuce cabbage etc.

Stones

Layer of gravel

Broken flower pot or similar for shelter.

Snails and Slugs: These are easy to catch in the garden after rain. If you are going to keep them in the classroom for a few days, what sort of home will they need? A vivarium - a glass tank with a top on - is ideal. How can the children find out what food they need? Encourage them to experiment with different leaves near where the creatures were found. Slugs and snails like to come out after the rain, so that means they want a damp environment. How will the children recreate this? A saucer full of water? A jar of water with some gauze over the top? What happens to the water? Where does it go? (See page 58.)

Let the children observe how snails and slugs move when they are climbing up the glass sides and watch them eating. Can they hear the rasping of their jaws? Watch them as they move across some paper. Why do they think they leave a slimy trail? If the children have been studying in groups, they could give a combined description of all they have found out about snails and slugs, including the difference between them.

What can we do if snails and slugs start eating all our lettuce in the garden? Children will probably suggest poisoning them with slug pellets. But what if other creatures eat the pellets, such as thrushes, who eat snails? Get them to experiment with barriers. What don't the slugs and snails like to crawl over? Sand? Sawdust? Chalk? Soot?

POND CREATURES

Making a Pond: Even if there is a limited space in your school grounds, making a pond is well worthwhile. It will provide a home for many creatures and plants as well as being a focal point for birds. The main principle is to line the dug-out area with a layer of thick newspapers, an old carpet or sieved sand to cover any sharp objects which might puncture the liner and then to spread a sheet of thick polypropylene on top, which will overlap the edges when filled with water. The liner should be covered with a layer of sand or earth and the edges weighed down with smooth stones. Be very careful not to tear or puncture the liner - the tiniest hole could mean loss of water and wildlife. At least a bucket full of water should be drawn from a natural pond, in order to introduce some pond life.

What will you put in your Pond: Take the children to a natural pond to find out as much as possible about the habitat. They might want to make some nets before they go to collect some of the pond life. They could then take a small amount of frog or toad spawn back to their own pond or a freshwater aquarium; also pond snails which keep the water clean. How could they prepare the pond or tank for when the tadpoles turn into adults?

Pond Diary: Older children could make a diary of their pond; younger children a picture book diary

DESIGNING THE POND

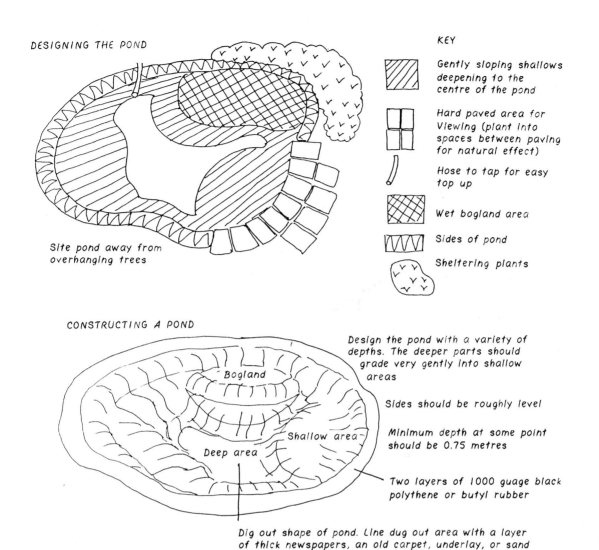

Site pond away from overhanging trees

KEY

Gently sloping shallows deepening to the centre of the pond

Hard paved area for viewing (plant into spaces between paving for natural effect)

Hose to tap for easy top up

Wet bogland area

Sides of pond

Sheltering plants

CONSTRUCTING A POND

Bogland

Shallow area

Deep area

Design the pond with a variety of depths. The deeper parts should grade very gently into shallow areas

Sides should be roughly level

Minimum depth at some point should be 0.75 metres

Two layers of 1000 guage black polythene or butyl rubber

Dig out shape of pond. Line dug out area with a layer of thick newspapers, an old carpet, underlay, or sand first removing large stones

Bogland area- including some tall plants for Dragonflies

CROSS-SECTION OF A WILDLIFE POND

Marginal plants

Oxygenating plants

Paving stone access in one or two areas

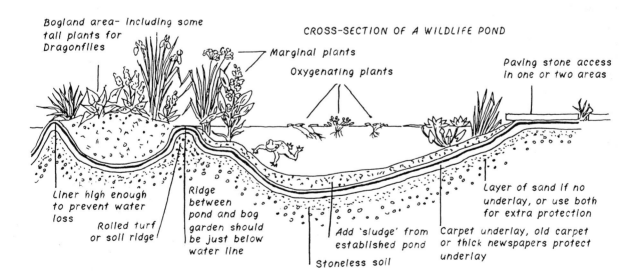

Liner high enough to prevent water loss

Rolled turf or soil ridge

Ridge between pond and bog garden should be just below water line

Stoneless soil

Add 'sludge' from established pond

Carpet underlay, old carpet or thick newspapers protect underlay

Layer of sand if no underlay, or use both for extra protection

with captions. How was it made and what has happened since then? What creatures were introduced? Which ones came of their own accord? Were there any problems? Did the water leak? Did some creatures eat others? What happens if duckweed is introduced?

If you have no pond in the grounds, seasonal visits could be made to one in the neighbourhood and the diary could record the changes observed. This should include the plants in and near the water and any bird life that is seen in or near the pond.

41

BIRDS

The best way for children to observe bird life is to build their own bird table, if possible within viewing distance of the classroom window. This will provide a basis for further studies when the children go out to explore their habitats.

Bird Tables: In designing a bird table, what do they need to take into consideration? What height would it have to be so that the birds could be watched from the window? How will they prevent the food from falling off? How will they remove mouldy food and clean the table? What about water? What could happen when it rains? Some smaller birds don't get a chance to eat their seeds; how could the big birds be prevented from clearing the board?

Young children could do simple sketches. Older children attempt to build their designs. Alternatively, the finished design could be entrusted to a handy parent. Children of all ages could suggest various extras: strings of peanuts in their shells, net bags and yoghurt pots filled with maize or hardened fat.

Bird Watching: Make an observation chart for making notes of the birds that visit the bird table. What are the most frequent visitors? Which are the rare ones? How do they fly to the table? Are they timid or aggressive? A graph could be compiled of the different birds, showing how many of each species are there in a given time and when they come.

What do Birds like to Eat: The children can try putting down a long tray, with several containers of different seeds, to find out which birds prefer which food. They could treat some of the seeds with non-toxic colouring to see if they show any colour preference. All of these findings can be tabulated and recorded. Children can explain the experiments to you or to others.

SCHOOL PLAYGROUNDS

Many playgrounds are nothing more than an area of solid concrete. However, with a little imagination they can still be transformed. Raised beds can be built up using old railway sleepers and filled with topsoil. Tall

flowes or vegetables can be grown in them, with climbers behind to hide bare walls. Hanging plants can drape themselves over the sides. If sleepers are not readily available, parents may be persuaded to try their hand at bricklaying!

Gro-bags can produce crops of tomatoes, radishes, carrots, or runner beans, all of which most children enjoy. However, these must be planned so that the holidays do not occur just when they ripen or are ready to be picked. Tubs, window boxes and containers can all make the playground a more pleasant place to be in and, if the children are responsible for their plants, they will take care that they are not vandalised by others, who might also have their own special plants to look after.

Environmental Playgrounds: More and more schools are obtaining funding from the local community to re-structure an area of concrete or a piece of wasteland. In the past, children's opinions have not been sought, but if they are consulted you may find that it gives them vision as well as more confidence.

Even very young children can give their opinions on what they would like: a safe area, play apparatus, an outside house, a garden. They can be interviewed using a tape recorder, simulating a TV or radio programme. Older children may be more ambitious and opt for planting trees, making a pond, growing vegetables, or having a wild flower area. They can formulate a questionnaire to ascertain pupils' choices and make a graph of it. Although they can let their imagination run riot on imaginary play areas and can write, paint, do murals and make plays about them, they will need to be guided in order to differentiate between fantasy and reality, just as they will have to co-operate in agreeing on the final outcome.

This needs to be a whole-school project with consideration given to every age level. Plans can vary from simple ideas of what we would see if we were in a helicopter, to scale drawings for the older ones. Modelling in Plasticine, clay or cardboard can give an idea of the layout and a miniature model on a large tray, with gravel, earth and tiny cardboard plants and play apparatus, can be a collaborative effort.

Research for the Play Space: Get the children to carry out a survey of what goes on in the playground. What do they want to keep? What causes problems? For example, a football field that takes up the whole of the play space. They can make a timetable of who uses the playground and for what. Are the girls or the boys ever deprived of space? Are the younger ones at a disadvantage? How could these problems be resolved? Again, this could be in the form of a questionnaire.

The Newcastle Architectural Workshop, 6 Higham Place, Newcastle-upon-Tyne, NE1 8AF, has been helping schools to formulate projects on nature playgrounds and their literature provides many more ideas.

The Size of the Play Space: The children can measure the area available with steps and then measure their step and check with a measuring tape or wheel.

Wildlife: Is there any wildlife in the playground? (Birds, insects, butterflies.) What would they like to attract in the new playground? Let them plan what trees, shrubs and flowers can go into a part of the playground.

The Five Senses: Encourage the children to plan their playground so that it appeals to all five senses: the colour of the flowers, the scent of herbs and blossoms, the song of the birds, the touch of the bark of trees or the feel of a piece of sculpture, and the taste of vegetables that could be grown.

CHAPTER V
THE SCHOOL AND THE COMMUNITY

Schools are working more and more with their local communities, building relationships, not only with parents but also councils and other agencies; and nowhere is this more important than the area of environmental education. Issues that are particularly relevant to young children are safety, provision for play, and access to the local natural environment: parks, commons, etc. Children should be able to visit special facilities such as nature centres, city farms and nature trails.

Positive action in the Community: We may sometimes feel powerless when faced with all the disasters that threaten the world but it is important for children to know that we can do something about them and that they can help in all sorts of ways, not least by giving a good example to others. They can clear litter; they can economise on energy; they can help to save paper and thus make a small contribution to the conservation of forests; they can help to recycle everything that can be used again; they can promote wild areas so that fewer creatures and plants will be deprived of a habitat, and they can make their voices heard about the species and peoples that are under threat, so that when they grow older, they will be better prepared to act as responsible citizens.

Home and School Working Together: Environmental education is an ideal reason for close co-operation between parents and teachers and where a whole-school approach is particularly valuable. Many parents are saying already that their children are reproaching them for throwing away bottles or for using aerosols! This communication, if pursued with tact, can be turned to good effect by a two-way system of mutual help: the school may provide the bottle bank or paper collection and parents can provide all sorts of materials for recycling and experimenting, and together they can ask the council for more local provision.

Keen gardeners in the local community may be willing to provide seeds and cuttings or even care for pot plants in the holidays and weekends. In return, they can be invited to tea parties, with homemade bread, fruit and nut biscuits and even school-grown herb tea.

44

DIY enthusiasts also come in handy. Their help with sawing, hammering and drilling and other potentially dangerous tasks can be invaluable. They might also be persuaded to lend a hand with the construction of a pond, raised beds in the playground or a wildlife area, and they can help to cultivate vegetables in the school garden or allotment. A joint sale of the produce could provide much needed funds for the extra materials suggested in this book, such as microscopes, magnifying glasses, aquaria and plants. School visits are often made possible by the co-operation of parents, who can help with small groups and generally support teachers, but parental help is equally invaluable in the classroom.

Invite parents into school from time to time to see what pupils are doing with regard to the environment. Sharing can help to promote mutual values with regard to caring for the natural world. And remember, joint action between home and school in the community can have a profound effect on policies formulated by local authorities and other influential bodies.

GETTING TO SCHOOL

Road Safety: A high proportion of pedestrian accidents involving children occur on school journeys. What do the children think about the traffic on the road today? Does it go too fast? Are they afraid of getting run over? Are there too many heavy lorries? What about wildlife: is it affected by more motorways and traffic?

Invite your local road safety officer into school to discuss some of these questions. How could roads be made safer? Special lanes for cyclists? More lollipop people?

Get the children to carry out a survey of the different ways they travel to school. How many don't walk? Is it because it is too far or too dangerous? Why should we walk to school if it is an option? Reasons could include: exercise, conserving energy if the journey would otherwise have been made by car/bus. How else can traffic be harmful?

Traffic Noise: Supervising children carefully, let them make tape recordings of the traffic near the school. Which are the noisiest vehicles? Can anything be done to cut down the noise?

Traffic Count: They can also make a traffic count, recording the number of cars, lorries, buses and bicycles that go by in a given time, and record the results on a graph. Do they have any suggestions on how the traffic could be cut down? Did they notice any fumes from the vehicles? Where did the fumes come from? Tell the children about catalytic exhaust cleaners.

In the Olden Days: What was it like before there were many cars? Children could interview elderly people in the community and find out what it was like when they were young. How did they get to school? Questions could be planned out beforehand with each group submitting a question.

NATURE TRAILS

Although there are numerous official nature trails, it is often more appropriate for young children to have their own specially designed venture. They can begin with the immediate surroundings of the school, once the grounds or (concrete playground!) have been well explored, identifying natural and man-made things and making a list of them back in the classroom. They can distinguish between modern and older buildings and get a feel for what the town or village was like a hundred or fifty years ago. Older children can interview elderly local inhabitants using their own questionnaires. Was there more greenery? Were there more places to play? What was school like?

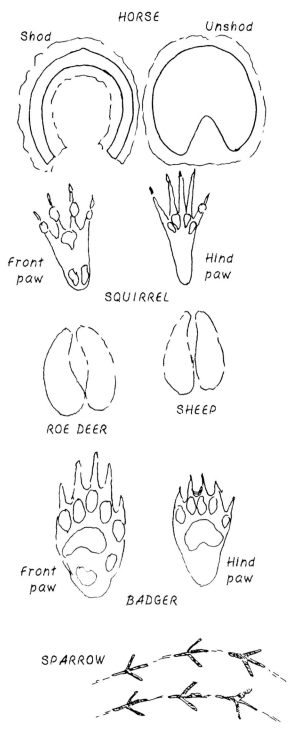

Animal Detectives: Besides footprints, children can also look for evidence of insects attacking leaves, remains of food, feathers, skeletons, animal droppings, pellets discarded by birds of prey, broken snail shells, old birds' nests, broken birds' eggs, spiders' webbs, and squirrels dreys. Can they tell what creatures have been there?

BOTANIC GARDENS

A visit to a botanic garden is the nearest most of us will get to experiencing the tropics. There are now more than thirty botanic gardens in Britain, so its worth consulting a map to see if you are near enough to one of them to make a visit. School parties are usually welcomed and there are sometimes staff who are able to work with the teachers.

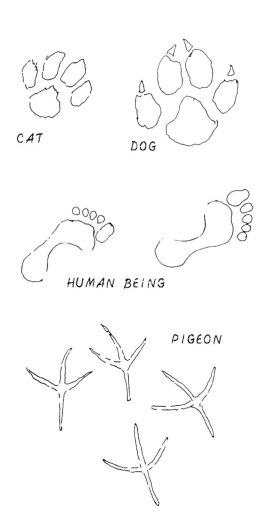

Nature Trail to School: First, the children should feel free to comment on anything that catches their attention. Then they could choose a different theme every day, with their parents' co-operation: for example, trees, flowers, gardens, walls. They could report to their classmates on what they have seen.

Animal Footprints Trail: Choose a damp day and a quiet place, perhaps near a pond, in a wood, or at a muddy farm to go looking for animal footprints. Alternatively, you need to wait until it snows.

Flower Trail: How many flowers are from the rainforests? The children can make sketches or take photographs of some of the exotic flowers in the hot houses.

Banana Trail: If there is a banana house, they could plan an imaginary trip to the Caribbean. They will notice that the bananas on the trees are green and that this is how they are picked. Why is this? (For the follow-up, there is dramatic representation on pages 56–59 in "World Studies, 8-13", which can be adapted for the younger age group; it gives a complete picture of the banana trade from cultivation to the greengrocer's shop in Britain.) Back in the classroom, they can paint banana palms, make clay models of bunches of bananas - and eat bananas!

Fruit Trail: Any exotic fruit can be treated in the same way, provided there are examples in the botanic garden: pineapples, orange and lemon trees are often to be seen. Again, give children the chance to taste the fruit being studied if it is something with which they are not familiar. The theme could be extended to include any foodstuffs we get from abroad, for example, spices, cocoa, coffee, sugar, and this visit could be linked with a study on food from the rainforests. (See page 72.)

Tree Trail: A tree-spotting walk can be fun. Children can invent names to describe the exotic trees that they find amongst the indigenous ones and then back in the classroom use books to find out the real names.

Multi-cultural Experience: Many children in our schools have parents who originate from the Caribbean, the Indian sub-continent, or Africa, and many of the botanic gardens have plant houses with specimens from these areas. Take the opportunity to forge links between the cultures by helping the children towards a greater understanding of all the benefits in the form of food and medicines that we get from these countries. Some parents might be able to accompany the class on these visits and they could supplement the experience with their own memories, either during the expedition or later in the classroom, when they could talk about the plant and animal life in their country of origin. They might even bring goodies like banana cake, sweet potatoes or mangoes for the children to sample.

FARM VISITS

Farm visits can stimulate much classroom activity, both before and after the experience. If it's an old family-run farm, the children might ask how things have changed. There could be simple role-plays with the "animals" saying which they preferred, life on the farm now, or in times past. Horses might think it was a good thing to have tractors; cows might prefer being milked by machine. But are there as many meadows to graze in? A number of farms cater for visits by school children.

City Farms: There are a growing number of city farms all over Britain and many of them welcome parties of school children. There are usually some animals selected for their appeal to children, such as rabbits, as well as goats, cows, sheep, pigs, etc. A half-day visit or shorter is recommended for young children. For many urban children and their parents, who might come along to help, it will be their first experience of a farm. Further information can be obtained from the National Federation of City Farms Ltd, The Old Vicarage, 66 Fraser Street, Windmill Hill, Bedminster, Bristol, BS3 4LY.

The Commonwork Land Trust: This is a wonderful place to visit: there are herds of cows, with liquid plant food being made on the spot from their manure; there are opportunities to make bread or do some pottery; to go on nature trails and a host of other activities. Further information can be obtained from The Education Project Co-ordinator, The Commonwork Land Trust, Bore Place, Chiddingstone, Edenbridge, Kent, TN8 7AR.

RECYCLING

People use up so much of the planet's wealth that we should all be responsible for trying to conserve it. Children need to be taught - and shown - that to maintain the natural balance on Earth we must restore the things we have taken from it. Children can readily understand this concept and can easily become the catalysts for conserving the planet, with the emphasis first on conservation, then on re-using, and finally on recycling.

Recycling Quiz: Give children a card with five recycling ideas on it. They should write in the name of the person who qualifies as having done one of the following tasks. There should be only one person against each item.

Find a person who has:

taken a bottle to the bottle bank ....
made something out of a plastic box ....
collected litter from the school grounds ....
brought something for the class junk box ....
refused packaging which was unnecessary ....

The children can add to these tasks with their own ideas. Younger children could do something similar orally - they would need a duplicated pictogram with drawings of suitable activities and classmates' names to tick off.

Creating a Recycling Machine: Older children can create an imaginary recycling machine in small groups. They would first need to talk about what sorts of things could be recycled, including ones that are not able to be recycled at the moment. The aim is to get the children thinking in a lateral way and to understand the needs of recycling, more than coming up with a realistic design. They might come up with a machine to flatten aluminium tins, so that they could be made into little trays.

How could they tell people about it and get them to

bring their tins? There are plenty of opportunities for role play here. (Acknowledgements to Karen Coulthard for the inspiration for these activities in "Green Teacher", September 1988.)

Sorting out the Dustbin: It is too unhygienic to sort out a real dustbin, so you can prepare one with various tins, garden rubbish, old newspapers, tin foil, vegetable peelings in a sealed bag, plastic containers, etc. Each group can have a turn at sorting out a "dustbin": putting the bottles on to different hoops and then into containers, according to the colour of the bottles; sorting the paper to be recycled; sorting tins with a magnet; saving the containers, and giving ideas for re-use in school.

School Recycling Unit: The school could set an example by having a recycling unit on site. This would be a whole-school activity and could encourage parents to co-operate in the project. You would need to arrange for a series of bins to be positioned in a safe place in the playground: one for paper that can be recycled, one for aluminium tins and foil, and another for stainless steel (having been sorted by the children by means of magnets. Often this magnet-sorting is done at the dump, but it is good practice for children to separate the metals and to find that aluminium is not attracted to the magnet, and also that it can be recycled in a different process from the stainless steel). There should be three bottle bins, one for green, one for brown and one for transparent bottles. If any bottles can be re-used, like milk bottles, they should be washed and returned. A further bin could be used for compost: rotting vegetables and fruit, lawn cuttings and garden waste, but not meat. It is a good idea to have a bin for non-biodegradable rubbish, as this would show children what to avoid in shopping. For example, at present plastic is too difficult to recycle on a reasonable scale, so this bin could be full of plastic bags and packaging. The children can paint on the bins indicating what they are for, with illustrations and labels. Contact your local recycling unit to see if they are able to collect this well-sorted waste. The garden refuse will go on the compost heap.

Plastic Rubbish: We use far too much plastic. It is a great threat to marine life as it is often tipped into the sea and takes hundreds of years to decompose. The children could brainstorm all the things that they use which are made of plastic. Can they think of anything they could use instead? For example, take a basket or a bag for shopping instead of carrier bags; use glass bottles for soft drinks instead of plastic and then re-use or recycle the bottle.

"Lateral" Recycling: Each child is given a common object and asked to think of other uses it could be put to, after it has been finished with; for example, tin cans can be adapted into stilts; plastic bottles make ideal flower vases and can be used for nature experiments in schools. Brainstorm all the articles that have been recycled by the class in carrying out any of the activities in this book.

Recycling in the Local Community: What recycling facilities are available in the vicinity of the school? You might be able to arrange for the children to visit a recycling centre. What can we recycle if it is collected regularly? Using a questionnaire, children can ask local people if they recycle their waste. If they do not, what prevents them? What would they like the council to do to help? How many bottle banks, waste paper bins, tin banks, etc, should there be and where could they be placed?

The questionnaire might be carried out at the school gates. This could be a joint effort between the older and younger children: the young ones asking the questions and the older ones recording the answers in simple terms.

Demand for Waste Disposal: Using the information collected with the questionnaire, the children could make up a role-play about people going to the council to ask for more waste disposal facilities.

Design of Bottle Banks: Get the children to look at and photograph or draw their local bottle banks.

Could they improve on the design, perhaps making ones which blend in more with the environment? They could do the same with litter bins. What colour should they be?

THE FUTURE

What kind of World do we want to live in?: Children are often worried by all the prophecies of doom and gloom. Unlike previous generations they cannot escape the anxieties expressed so continually on television. This book tries to instil a love and respect for all things in the natural world as a basis for future practical concern and care for the planet.

In this way, children will begin to feel more in charge of their own future. They can also develop a feeling of the sequence of the past, present and future.

Time Lines: Get the children to draw a line and mark on it when they were born and where we are now. They can paste in photographs of themselves during that time in sequence, or draw pictures of incidents in their life that they specially remember. It might be a birthday party, moving house, Christmas, or other celebrations; it might be something sad, like the death of a pet. Older children can mark in the years and note the major events that took place.

Future Time Lines: Using their time line, can they continue it to show what they think will happen to them in the future? What would they like to do when they grow up? Older children can draw two lines from age 7 or 8: one "What I think might happen to me" and the other, "What I would like to happen to me."

The Planet's Future: For older children a time line on "What I would like to happen to the planet by the year 2000" could be appropriate, for example:-

Things which Change: Brainstorm all sorts of things that can change: things that were once in their house or flat; things that change slowly/quickly. Have their clothes changed? Their food? Friends? Where they live?

Things that they have Changed: Have they changed their appearance? Done something to help somebody? Made something more beautiful? Children can talk about changes in themselves that they are happy about: "I used to ... but now ...". Ask

Rainforest saved	No wars
No more acid rain	Less noise
Protect birds, whales, butterflies, frogs etc.	No harmful chemicals
Humans, trees and animals saved from pollution	

When I grow up: Discuss what children want to be when they grow up. They can look through magazines to cut out pictures of anything representing their job. Very young children could simply cut out pictures. Older children can paste them on to a board and comment on their choice of picture and why they are interested in that particular job. Which jobs are usually outdoors? Which jobs help others? Which jobs deal with children? Older children can make a pictogram of the choices of members of their group.

What do I Remember?: This exercise can help children to get in touch with their own past by remembering earlier events from their lives and creating "storyboards" of what they remember. What is their earliest memory? What was their first day at nursery or school like? What did they like to play when they were ... years old? What do they recall about any holidays? Days out? Birthdays? The storyboard should consist of a large piece of drawing paper divided into six squares with the title, "I Remember", and a drawing in each in sequence. Older children can include a sentence describing what they remember.

them to list the changes in what they do now, compared with when they were younger.

Time Capsule: Explain to the class that a time capsule is a collection of souvenirs chosen for what they reveal about a group of people, like themselves, at a certain time. It is then buried, only to be opened by people in the future who want to learn about their predecessors. It could, of course, be buried in the school grounds and be dug up at the end of the school year! What sort of souvenirs would they like to include? If the items are too big, like a television set, what could they do about that?

A Beautiful World of the Future: Children of all ages could contribute to a large mural showing a beautiful world that they would like to live in when they are grown up. Older children could make two contrasting pictures: one of the world of their dreams and the other depicting a barren polluted landscape, full of motorways and factories but no trees, parks or any kind of greenery.

CHAPTER VI
THE NATURAL WORLD

How much do children really know about topical environmental issues? What do they think the greenhouse effect is? What about the hole in the ozone layer? Acid rain? Rainforest destruction? Children need to know how dependent we are on the physical world and yet how vulnerable that world is. They only need simple explanations at this stage and to know that people, including themselves, can do something to improve the situation. The most disturbing factor for young children is to feel that adults are powerless and cannot protect them. It is up to you to decide how much of this information is suitable for your pupils.

For the very young, the experience of the basic elements of the natural world is the foundation for future care and understanding, and in this chapter the activities lead children progressively towards a deeper insight into the power of the forces of nature and our need to treat them with respect.

THE EARTH IN SPACE

Children today are bombarded with spacemen, space games, spaceships and space stories and are fascinated by the idea of space exploration. They are ready for simple explanations of night and day, the seasons and the stages of the moon, as long as they are acted out and accompanied by visual models.

Near and Far: As a preliminary exercise, look at photographs showing how people and buildings look smaller the further away they are: children in the forefront can look taller than the adults; houses, cars and trees can look tiny when they are in the background. In the same way, you can explain to the children that the sun is much, much bigger than our tiny earth, but it looks quite small because it is so far away.

Sun and Earth: Take two large pieces of white card and cut out two equal circles. Get the children to work out how to do this. Then, in small groups, they take it in turns to colour the circles in yellows, reds and oranges with great swirls. Other groups can be preparing cut-out flames to stick round the painted circles. Two shoulder straps can be glued on to the insides of the circles, so that they will fit any child wearing them. Similar, much smaller circles can be made to represent the Earth, coloured blue and green, or a papier mache ball about 3cm in diameter can be fixed on to a thin stick or wire.

Day and Night: In a darkened room, one child wears the sun image and shines a strong torch on to a child who represents the Earth by revolving slowly to illustrate day and night. Everyone will probably want a turn as either the sun or moon, or both, and the repetition will help to consolidate the concept. A globe with an axis will make the distinction between night and day much clearer, as long as children are reminded that all the models of the Earth should be much smaller in comparison with the sun.

The Earth round the Sun: While the children are still wearing the models, ask the child representing the Earth to walk very slowly round the sun. Do the children know how long the complete circle takes in reality? They can repeat the earlier activity, "Day and Night", with the earth revolving on its axis at the same time as progressing very slowly round the sun (they don't have to do it 365 times!). Older children can make the orbit of the earth holding a globe, keeping its axis pointing to the North Pole. They can see that when it is tilted towards the sun, the days in the northern hemisphere are long and the nights short, which is our summer. When the North Pole is tilted away from the sun, the days are short and the nights

long, which is our winter. These are difficult concepts to grasp, but repeated experiences such as those suggested above should make them clearer and interesting at the same time. A visit to a planetarium is worthwhile as long as it is well prepared beforehand.

Moon round the Earth: It is best to use the globe for the Earth and make a small papier mache white ball with a stick stuck in it, to represent the moon. A child stands in the centre, holding the globe (which is revolving) and another child walks slowly round it, holding the moon on the stick, making a complete circle for each month. Twelve children could do this, one at a time, to make the months of the year. Once again, they enjoy the repetition and this will consolidate the cycle in their minds.

LIFE ON EARTH

Children are intrigued by the idea of extra terrestrial beings. Answering the imagined questions of these strangers is just one way to give the children a whole new perspective on our lives on earth.

Aliens: What do children think an alien would look like? According to what they decide, one child could dress up as an alien who wants to know about our planet and ask the rest of the class what humans are like. What about animals, plants, cars, etc? This could be a regular feature with a different theme each time and the children taking it in turns to be the alien. This gives pupils important practice in posing questions and thinking for theselves as well as describing as accurately as possible the objects and processes that the beings want to know more about. Younger children could begin with the teacher as the alien, so that they get the idea of the questioning; then everyone takes turns.

Spaceship: They are going on a long journey to outer space. What would they take with them? What would they take to show other beings what Earth was like? A large spaceship could be drawn on card fixed to the wall and the children could pack it by sticking in objects to illustrate life on Earth. The children should decide what to take. Some ideas might be: photographs, the cover of a book, pictures of trees and animals, musical instruments and food.

Modelling the Globe: Children can blow up a balloon and cover it with papier mache; let it dry out then let the balloon down and paste over the hole. They need to colour it in green for the land and blue for the oceans. Older children could give a more accurate picture of the continents. Encourage them to look at photographs of the Earth taken from the moon.

Globe Spotting: Children are fascinated with globes of the Earth, especially the inflatable ones and those with an electric light inside. In groups, they can take turns in identifying parts of the Earth, with the older ones using their more detailed knowledge of countries and oceans.

The Planets: With the model sun in the centre, each child can be a planet, walking slowly round the sun. The children should understand that our Earth is only one of the planets going round the sun: there are eight more that we know of, and maybe more that we haven't yet discovered. Mercury is the nearest to the sun, then Venus, Earth, Mars, Jupiter, Saturn, Uranus, Neptune and Pluto. The myths of Rome can be told, so that the children know where these names come from: for example, Venus was the goddess of love, Mars the god of war, Jupiter the king of the gods, Mercury the messenger of the gods, Saturn a god of the Earth, Uranus of astronomy, Neptune the god of the sea, and Pluto the god of the underworld.

Planet Models: As technology develops, scientists are discovering more and more about the planets surrounding the sun. Space travel attracts a lot of publicity in the media and children will enjoy collecting this on video or from newspapers and magazines. Children can make models of the planets in papier mache or clay, using balloons or inflatable spheres for the largest, like Jupiter and Saturn. Papier mache models can be hung up as a mobile round the sun, with Saturn surrounded by its ring of moons. Alternatively, the planets can be represented on a wall chart, either by drawings or small scale models, with rings round the sun at approximate distances. These exercises are more suitable for older children.

Photographs of the Planets: Photographs of the planets taken from satellites are a source of wonder and great beauty. You will find them in most good reference books. Children could paint colourful pictures of them.

SUNSHINE AND SHADOWS

Catching Shadows: Each pair of children has a lightweight board on which to draw the outline of any shadow they can "catch" - maybe a plant, a pot or a toy. They can then colour it with chalks. It will

not be the same shape as the object that is casting the shadow; it may be quite tiny at midday and very long in the late afternoon. Can they say why this is?

Changing Shadows: In pairs, at various times during the day, children can observe the shadows cast by a stick fixed to the ground and see how they change. They can chalk the outline of the various positions of the shadow and find out the pattern of the movement. What is it that is moving? Do they notice when the shadow is darker? Lighter? They could do the same with shadows of a partner, chalking their silhouette on the playground at regular intervals throughout the day. The partner must remember to stand on exactly the same spot each time.

Making a Sundial: See if you can arrange to take the children to see a sundial. Can they work out how to make a simple one of their own? What does it need to show what time it is? A clock face can be made out of white cardboard and marked with the hours. What could make the shadow? A stick secured with Plasticine is one idea. How would they know if the shadow was pointing to the right time? (References: Gore, S "My Shadow"; Roth, S "The Story of Light.")

CELEBRATING THE SEASONS AND CHANGING NATURE

The concept of change in the natural world is not always easy for young children to grasp: mountains seem to be everlasting and the sea a permanent stretch of water. In this section a look at the seasons, which bring about "natural" change, leads on to a study of some of the man-made changes and the treats they pose to our environment. Changes According to the Seasons: What changes do the children make according to the season? Clothes? Play? What are the main changes in plant and tree life? What changes do animals make? (Hibernation, migration, change of coat, etc.)

Spring: The coming of spring is welcomed in many countries: in parts of Britain, May Day is celebrated with garlands and maypoles. Can the children design a model maypole? It could be made simply with bamboo and streamers. Can they learn some maypole dances?

More recent innovations include Earth Day on 22nd April, celebrating our awareness of the needs of the planet and World Environment Day on 5th June when whole schools can do something collectively to care for the earth.

Summer: Midsummer Day, on 24th June is three days after the longest day in the northern hemisphere and is the source of many fairy stories of mysterious happenings. Do the children know of any, or could they find some out?

Autumn: Harvest festivals are widely celebrated. Children can bring fruit, flowers and vegetables to give thanks for the fruitfulness of the Earth. They can cut up fruit or vegetables to make a huge fruit salad or vegetable soup for the class.

One World Week is celebrated at the end of October and aims to foster recognition of common needs throughout the world. Children should be encouraged to consider the cost in human terms of the varied and plentiful diet we enjoy and remember the plight of others who do not have enough.

Divali is the Festival of Lights celebrated at the end of October or the beginning of November. Children can make little clay oil lamps; these are lit and placed in every window in India to celebrate the Goddess of Plenty, Lakshmi.

Winter: St Nicholas' Day is on December 6th and for many children in Europe it is like Christmas, with presents and feasting.

AIR

All living creatures need air; humans and animals breathe in oxygen and breathe out carbon dioxide, so do plants when there is no light. When plants are in the sun they do the opposite: taking in carbon dioxide and giving out oxygen. This is a good example of interdependence. We need the oxygen from plants, they use the carbon dioxide we breathe out.

Deep Breathing: The children should lie on the floor and breathe through their nose to the count of three, hold their breath for the same count, and then expel it through the mouth, again to the count of three. This is a relaxing exercise which helps to encourage the healthy practice of breathing from the diaphragm; this should be emphasised by getting the children to put their hands on their stomachs to feel the rise and fall as they breathe in and out.

Count your Breath: Get the children to count how many times they breathe in and out in one minute, timed by a classmate. Then get them to do some vigorous exercise, like jumping up and down or running fast round the hall, and count how many breaths per minute they take after the exercise. Why do they think it is quicker?

How do we know that Air is there?: If we can't see air, how do we know that it is there? Do the children know of any games that are based on blowing balloons or feathers in a race? Could they make up a game like this? For example, each child could have a narrow tube and a feather: how far can they blow the feather in one go? How can they bring back the feather without touching it? Is the wind air? How can they tell?

Capturing Air: Children love to blow up balloons and let them go. What makes them go so quickly? Why do they make a noise? Older children could be challenged to think of a way in which a balloon could make a truck move. How could we weigh air? It would have to be contained in some way: paper bags,

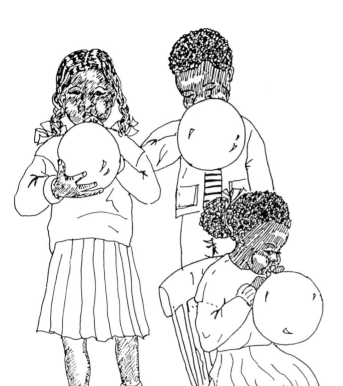

AIR POLLUTION

The air we breathe is becoming increasingly polluted, causing widespread damage to our health, to wildlife and to the whole equilibrium of the planet.

Acid Rain: Hundreds of tonnes of polluting gases, like sulphur dioxide, nitric oxide and nitrogen dioxide, enter the atmosphere every day from our cars, factories and power stations. They rise up and combine with water to form dilute acid, which falls as rain. Acid rain pollutes lakes and rivers, strips trees of their leaves, destroys nutrients in the soil and eats away historic buildings and statues.

The Ozone Layer: Between 20 and 50 kilometres above the earth is a thin layer of oxygen-related gas called ozone, which filters out 99% of the ultra-violet radiation of the sun. This ozone is slowly being destroyed by chlorofluorocarbons or CFCs and scientists have discovered a large hole in the ozone layer above the frozen Antarctic and a smaller one above the Arctic. This means that we are exposed to more of the ultra-violet in the sun's rays.

Ultra-violet radiation is thought to contribute to skin cancer and the destruction of plankton in the ocean. Plankton produces oxygen, which creatures in the sea need to breathe. CFCs are found in many aerosols, cartons made of polystyrene and refrigerators. It is vital that CFCs are no longer used in the manufacture of these goods; in the meantime the public should refuse to buy them.

Low level ozone is a serious pollutant which can increase dramatically when dangerous chemicals emitted from car exhausts and certain industrial processes react with sunlight. These chemicals are

balloons? The children would need a balance to weigh the bags of air. Give them some string, wire coat hangers, strips of dowelling, Plasticine, and see what they come up with. Why would the containers of air have to be the same size? This can lead to the notion of a fair test.

Movements of Air: Ask the children to guess what will happen if a down feather is placed above a hot radiator? Were they right? They could try with other objects: a small piece of tissue paper, a balloon. Does it work with slightly heavier objects, like a postcard or a small square of cotton? Encourage them to try the experiments on a cold radiator to confirm their conclusions.

Blowing Bubbles: Children love blowing bubbles; they would have fun experimenting with different sized rings to see which produces the biggest bubble. How hard must they blow? What happens if they blow too hard? If there is a hot radiator in the classroom, they can see what happens when the bubbles are directed towards it. Why is that?

unburnt hydrocarbons from oil-based products and nitrogen oxides. In the presence of sunlight they react to form low level ozone, creating smog, causing damage to crops and forests as well as people - it harms our lungs, makes us cough and gives us headaches.

Low Level Ozone Survey: "Watch" has carried out a survey with children to detect the level of ozone in the air using the tobacco plant, **Nicotiana Tabacum** which is "ozone sensitive". The seeds are planted and remain indoors for eight weeks and then are placed outside to monitor ozone. The leaves spot as they are affected by the ozone; the more ozone, the greater the number of spots. Although the survey has ended, "Watch" still supplies seeds of Nicotiana Tabacum with full details of the ozone level project; they also supply seeds of another Nicotiana which is not ozone sensitive and therefore acts as a control. The two species can be compared. The children could decide where to place the two pots of Nicotiana. How could they tell if the spots were not due to another cause, like blackspot? (See list of useful addresses on page 86).

Car Exhausts: Safety Note: This activity requires careful supervision. It is best for the teacher to demonstrate the experiment. You may need another adult's help to start up and sit in the car. Take a small group of older children to the school car park when it is quite safe. Hold filter paper against the exhaust of a running car to show children the dirt that comes out of most exhausts. The children could do a count of the vehicles passing the school and consider how much dirt would go into the atmosphere from them - in half an hour, in a day. When would the traffic be heaviest? (See page 49 on "Going to School".)

How else is our air polluted? Older children are becoming conscious of how dirty air affects people's lungs, especially babies, those who are ill and the elderly, so they can relate these activities directly to people's health.

Keeping our Air clean: Prepare simple cards describing ways of saving and wasting energy. Each child reads out one statement and asks the class if this will make the air cleaner or dirtier. 1. You walk to school. 2. You are driven to school. 3. You go by car with three other children. 4. You take a bus instead of a car. 5. You turn off the electric lights when it is light enough to see. 7. You leave the lights on in the classroom when you go out to play. 8. You use the washing machine for just a few clothes. 9. You put an extra jumper on instead of turning on the heating.

10. You jump about to keep warm rather than turning up the heating.

This could also be used as a questionnaire.

In a discussion afterwards, it will become clear that there are many decisions that children cannot make: there may be no buses to school and it may be too far, or too dangerous, to walk. Get them to suggest ways in which they can play their part in reducing pollution. If they have to go by car, can they have a rota with their classmates, thus saving several cars making the same journey? Can they walk using a rota system, so that one adult in turn accompanies a small group? How can they save electricity? Turning off lights and heating when it is not essential, wearing warmer clothes.

Pollution Test: The children can cut out some squares of absorbent paper and pin or stick them in various places around the school premises. They should collect them the next day and see if there is any dirt on them. Do some places produce more dirt than others? Look at the squares under the microscope and/or under a powerful magnifying glass. Can they count the biggest specks of dirt? Alternatively, sticky paper can be fixed to the various spots, sticky side upwards. Leaves can be collected and washed with detergent then the water passed through a filter, or they can be wiped with a clean, damp tissue paper while still growing. If a microscope is to be used, they can place two slides smeared with Vaseline outside the classroom, one in a box exposed to the elements and the other covered with a filter.

Testing for Acid Rain: Are plants affected by acid rain? How? What are the signs? Grow plants in compost in two containers and water one with tap water and the other with tap water with a small amount of vinegar added. What is the result? Can the children see any signs of acid rain in the trees in their neighbourhood?

A Mural of Acid Rain: Paint a picture to show factories and cars pouring out poisonous gases, which rise to form clouds, which then fall as rain on trees and buildings. A positive mural could be depicted alongside it, showing factories labelled with filter systems and cars fitted with catalytic convertors. If they have done the pollution test (see above), children will understand that some kind of filter system could take out some of the dirt. (References: Paychett, L "Clean Air, Dirty Air", A & C Black 1990. McCormick, J "Acid Rain", Franklin Watts 1985.)

EARTH

Children love to play with mud and make things out of clay. Modelling clay or sand is a creative exercise which can be highly therapeutic. Children also enjoy digging holes and making sand castles and although this cannot often take place in a natural environment, a large sand tray and, if possible, an equally large earth tray, will allow them to experiment with the properties of different kinds of soil. (Children should always wear gloves when handling soil).

Weighing: Can they design a balance to weigh earth? Does it have to be different to the balance they used to weigh air? If they use yoghurt pots, must they be the same size? They can experiment to see if the same amount of sand weighs more or less than clay. This can be checked on a weighing machine and older children can record the results. What else could they weigh? Wet sand and dry sand; pebbles and sand; compost and clay. Why are seeds grown in compost rather than clay? Sometimes they are grown in a mixture of sand and compost.

Soil Erosion: Older children could experiment with landscapes in the earth or sand trays. They could sprinkle rain near the top of a mountain (eg from a watering can) and watch what happens to the sand. How could they prevent the sand being swept away? If they plant "trees" (twigs), would that hold the sand together? Discuss what holds soil together and what happens if it is swept away. Do they think earth would be swept away more or less easily than sand? Were they right?

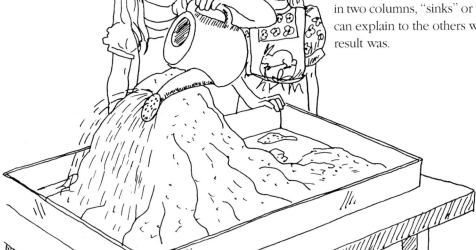

Archaeological Dig: If there is a small area of wasteland in the school grounds, organise a mini-dig. Make sure that the children all wear gloves. Take your finds back to the classroom and wash, weigh and record them. Pieces of crockery, unusual stones, pieces of cloth, metal objects, etc can sometimes be found. You might need to bury a typical selection of likely treasures beforehand. What has happened to paper and card? Discuss how our refuse is disposed of. What materials are bio-degradable?

Rock Collection: See if the class can collect different sorts of rocks: limestone, slate, granite, chalk, flint, etc. They can classify them into groups of the same kind. What other ways? Size, shape, colour? Parents may be able to help them with their collection which could be displayed on a table with appropriate labels. The display could also be examined through a powerful magnifying glass or a microscope, starting with a grain of sand. What differences are there between the grains? What colours? Where does sand come from?

WATER

Water is vital in every child's development and the following experiences can link their knowledge of the propensities of water to its role in their lives and the natural world.

Floating and Sinking: Children can experiment with a series of objects to see whether they sink or float: leaves, pebbles, wood, soap, sponges, a metal spoon, etc. Can the children guess which ones will float? Does Plasticine or clay sink? How could they make it float? They can put marbles in a boat and estimate how many can be put in before it sinks. Older children can make pictograms of their results in two columns, "sinks" or "floats". Younger children can explain to the others what they did and what the result was.

Evaporation: Taking the appropriate safety measures, boil a kettle of water. Ask the children what will happen to the steam if a cold plate is placed against it. Can evaporation always be seen? What does water need to evaporate? Can they think of a safe way to show that water evaporates? Try placing a saucer of water on a sunny window sill. How can they find out how much water has evaporated? If it is sea water, or water with salt added, what happens to the salt? How do we get sea salt?

Plant Evaporation: Can the children think of a way to show that plants transpire? There needs to be warmth and something to collect the moisture. They might tie a plastic bag round the plant and see if water appears on the plastic.

Watering Plants: Children know that they need to water their plants. How much should they water them? Desert plants, for example, need very little, as they store water in their leaves, whereas water pond plants, like the yellow water iris, need a lot.

How do Plants Drink?: Can they think of an experiment to show how plants drink through their roots and stems? If they put a stick of celery into a jar of coloured water, what will happen? You should be able to see the coloured water rising up the veins. Put some white flowers, such as carnations, into this solution and see what happens. (Note: Use non-toxic colouring.) If you split the stems and put half into differently coloured water, the flowers of each half would be of different colours.

How much do Plants Drink?: Older children can measure how much water a plant drinks. Put the stem of a busy lizzie into a measuring jug half-full of water. Mark the level and take readings daily and make a record of the results. Does the amount of water vary? Why? What would happen if all the water was used up?

Using Water: Ask the children what they use water for in their everyday lives. Can they work out how much they drink while they are at school? Older children can estimate first and then work out their consumption for one whole day. If it's possible, arrange a visit to a water treatment plant or sewage works or contact your local water authority for information.

There is often a shortage of water in this country, but in other countries it can be much more severe. Can the children think of ways in which they could use less water? How would they manage if they did not have water in their homes? What did people do when there was no running water? Children could interview older people. What do people do in countries where there is a permanent shortage of water? Let them try carrying a bucket of water across the playground. How many times can they manage to do this? How many metres would that be? Some people have to carry water for many kilometres. (References:

Parker, P "Water for Life". Development Education Centre, Birmingham 1990; Walpole, B "Water"; Ellis, C "Water". BBC Fact Finders 1990.)

SOIL AND WATER POLLUTION

The pollution of soil is linked directly to the pollution of water and ultimately the sea. Agricultural waste from toxic biocides, insecticides and fertilisers not only affect the wildlife in and around the soil but also seep into water courses, causing oxygen depletion and toxicity on land and sea. Wildlife is being affected, particularly at the top of the food chain - and this includes human beings (see page x). Sewage, full of household chemicals and industrial waste, penetrates into the earth and untreated sewage is frequently discharged into the seas. Industrial chemicals, oil and radioactive material are continually pumped into our rivers and oceans.

Measuring Water Pollution: Get the children to place beakers to collect rainfall in various parts of the school grounds, making sure that they are not under trees or roofs and away from buildings. They can collect the beakers after it has rained and put the water through a fine coffee filter, then look at the deposits through a magnifying glass and under a microscope. Are they the same as the ones collected from the air? (See page 66). Can they see all of the pollution in this way? How do the rain drops collect the pollution? They can send a sample away for testing to see what the rain that falls in your area contains. (See page 85 on Watch.)

Water Creatures: Can they make a list of all the creatures they can think of that live in or near the water? Some examples are: fish, tadpoles and frogs, ducks, whales, otters, water snails, water snakes, dolphins, herons, seals, puffins, guillemots - many of which are now at risk because from pollution. What happens to birds if there is an oil spillage at sea? How can they be saved?

THE WEATHER

Weather Symbols: Working in pairs, children can invent their own symbols for charting the weather: sunshine, half-cloud, overcast, light rain, heavy rain, hail, snow, etc. They can report to the others what their choice has been and why.

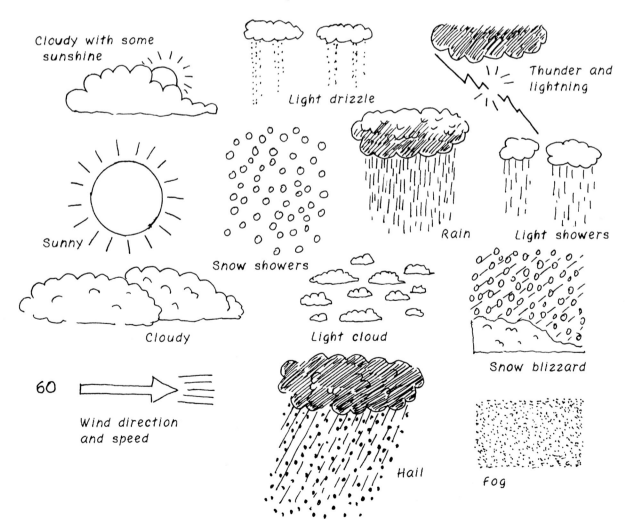

Cloudy with some sunshine

Light drizzle

Thunder and lightning

Sunny

Snow showers

Rain

Light showers

Cloudy

Light cloud

Snow blizzard

Wind direction and speed

Hail

Fog

Making a Weather Chart: Can the children design a weather chart? They could discuss what they need in small groups. One idea is to have a weekly one - Monday to Friday - drawing in the symbols each day; or they could make columns for the weather and just tick them off. Older children could think of a way of using their symbols such as making cards for them and experimenting with ways in which to attach them to the chart. Each day monitors could hang up the appropriate cards to describe the kind of weather.

Taking the Temperature: Children can compare indoor and outdoor temperatures every day at the same time with a special clearly marked thermometer. Why is it important to take them at the same time? Young children can decide whether the temperature is hot, warm or cold and then find out what the temperature is. Older children can guess what the temperature might be after they have had some experience of recording it. They can make comparisons as to whether it is warmer or colder than the day before or the week before.

A Simple Home-made Thermometer: Get the older children to observe carefully their classroom thermometer then see if they could make their own. Could they use water instead of mercury? How could they see it clearly? What could they use for the tube? A straw? How could they tell how much the water had risen? The diagram shows one idea of how to do this.

Forecasting the Weather: Children can listen to, or watch on television, the local weather forecasts for one week in the classroom. They can discuss the different symbols and compare them with their own. Were the forecasts right? It is best to study local programmes for greater simplicity and accuracy. Weather Sayings: How many weather forecast sayings can they collect? Families can help out with this, especially the older generations. Let them test them out when there is an opportunity.

Weather and the Seasons: What weather do they associate with the four seasons? Is it always true? eg snow in winter, showers in the spring, drought in summer, winds in autumn. Talk about the weather in the season that has just passed. Was it what they would have expected? What activities do they relate to the different seasons? How does the weather affect what we wear?

CLOUDS

Cloud Formations: Take the children outside and watch the clouds go by; if it is fine they can sit or lie on the ground. What are the clouds like? Imagine the clouds are animals. What are they? Usually there is a series of different shapes. In pairs, can the children identify two shapes, for example, a monster or a castle and make up a story about them.

Painting Clouds: Children can make a picture by first painting a blue sky and then dipping small cloud shapes cut out of sponge, in to thick white paint and pressing them over the blue paint. They can experiment with different effects. This can be an opportunity for older children to learn the different types of clouds and label them: for example, cumulus, stratus, and cirrhus.

What are Clouds?: Children will know that clouds can produce rain and that the heavier and darker the cloud, the more likely it is to rain. The exercises on evaporation and condensation will help them to understand the process (see page 58). What do they think happens when the clouds are high in the atmosphere? Do the droplets change? What are clouds like in high mountain areas?

Snow Flakes: If it snows, help the children collect some snow flakes on black velvet material, placed on ice cubes and quickly examine the ice crystals under a magnifying glass. Do the same using white material. What is the difference?

'Jack Frost': Look at the patterns that frost can make on window panes and cut out patterns like them out of folded paper.

Melting Ice: Let the children see how long it takes for an ice cube on a saucer on the radiator to melt. Compare it with one on the window sill. They could also weigh two equal cubes of ice, wrap one in black material and one in white and see which one melts first. Why is this?

RAIN

Feelings about Rain: Who likes rain? What do they dress in to protect themselves from the rain? What words can they think of to do with rain and hail? Can they make a class poem using some of the words?

Measuring Rainfall: How can they collect rain and find out how much has fallen? Younger children might think of just placing a container outside and pouring the rain water into a measuring jug. Would there be more water in a wider container? Let them try it. Older children might think of a funnel cut from the top of a plastic bottle, turned upside down to catch the water in the bottle.

How could they measure the amount each day? Could they use a plastic ruler? They should discuss where best to place the bottle. How will they stop it being blown over? Remind children that rain water is better than tap water for plants, so any water collected will really help their plants to grow.

Rainstorm: This is a popular activity which gives good experience of a co-operative effort. The children

sit in a circle with the leader in the middle. He/she makes the following movements and sounds and the others imitate her/him. First, rubbing hands together; then tiny claps (older children can snap their fingers); then slapping their legs with their hands and, at the height of the storm, stamping their feet. Here flashes of light from torches or the lights being switched on and off and the rumble of thunder (sound effects suggested by the children) could be introduced. Reverse the movements until the storm subsides.

THE WATER CYCLE

Ask the children where rain comes from. They may know it comes from clouds, but what kind of clouds drop the rain and where does it go? The clouds keep on forming and collecting more rain; where does it come from?

You can help children to understand that water turns into steam when it gets hot by boiling a kettle (safety, at a distance) then holding a cold plate over the steam. What happens? If the water can change into steam and then back to water again, how else can it change? Snow, ice, hail? What causes this?

If water needs to be heated to turn into water vapour, can the children think of other ways to show this, besides using a kettle of boiling water? Can the sun make the water hot? If they put a saucer of water in the sun, what happens? How can they measure it? Supposing they put salt in the water, what would happen? Encourage children to predict what will happen and then see if they were right.

From previous experiments (see page 58), the children should know that plants take up water through their roots and let it out through their leaves. This, and the water which evaporates from rivers and seas, rises to form clouds and eventually falls as rain. Explain to them that this whole process is called the water cycle. Older children might paint pictures or diagrams to illustrate what happens or even devise a model to demonstrate it.

RAINBOWS

Draw a Rainbow: Each child can draw a rainbow to help them learn the correct sequence of colours. They might look through prisms first to help them. When can we see a rainbow? Have the children ever seen rainbow colours anywhere else? What about in patches of oil spilt on the road?

RED
ORANGE
YELLOW
GREEN
BLUE
INDIGO
VIOLET

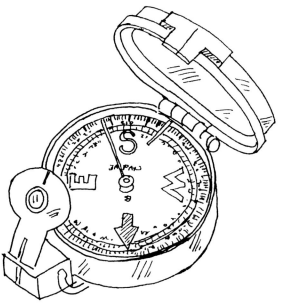

THE WIND

Wind Direction: How can children tell if the wind is blowing? They may not be able to see the wind but they can see bushes and trees swaying, and autumn leaves being swept about or clothes on the washing line blowing. Can they tell from what direction the wind is blowing? Talk about wind socks and weather vanes. Children could try putting a wet finger in the air and seeing which side dries first; holding a streamer in the air; putting up a flag.

The Points of a Compass: Young children can learn the four points of the compass, older ones should manage the eight points and then be able to say where the wind is coming from with its help.

Gales: How many children remember the gales we have had in recent years? Can they recall how they felt? What were they doing at the time? These memories could lead to some creative writing. What happened to the trees? What can we do about this? Some parks have raised money to replace the fallen trees with saplings. How long does it take for a tree to grow to its full height? Children can get some idea by counting the rings on mature trees that have been sawn down. (See page 36.)

Wind Power Can the children think of things that need wind to make them work, such as kites and windmills?

Making a Kite Can the children make their own kite? What sort of material will they need, light or heavy? If they use paper, what kind will it be? Can they make a kite out of metal? What about thin tinfoil, like some balloons? Or wood? (Balsa sticks for example). Have an assortment of materials for the children to experiment with: various kinds of paper, cloth, string, ribbons, wood, slats, thin wire, balsa wood glue, Sellotape, hole punch, etc. Discuss shape: what are some of the most common shapes for kites? Why are they that shape? If the paper is thin, how could the shape be held? How will they make the tail? How will they decorate it? Remind them it needs to be seen from the ground.

The illustration gives a simple idea of a kite made from slats of wood, paper and wire. The kites can be tested in the playground and if any do not fly, the

children can discuss likely reasons? (Too heavy a body or tail? Too short a string?) How could they remedy this? Children could write about "How I made my kite" and take a photograph or do an illustration of it.

Making a Windmill Can the children design and make a windmill? Materials to provide for them might include: two pint milk cartons, pieces of medium and thin wire, long nails, cotton reels, corks, balsa wood

sticks, thin bamboo sticks, paper of varying thickness, Sellotape and glue. How will they make the windmill stable?

The children could experiment in pairs, designing and making sails. How will they make them catch the wind? If a visit to a working windmill is possible, they can observe the flaps and add them to their models. Most children should manage to punch criss-cross sails together, but how will the sails be fixed to the mill? They need to turn freely on the wire. Two holes could be punched opposite each other at the top of the milk carton and the wire threaded through. How can they stop it from falling off? With Plasticine, a cork, a cotton reel?

The windmills will need to be tested in the playground when there is sufficient wind. Assessments and adjustments can then be made. The diagram shows one idea of how to make a windmill. A discussion could follow on wind power. What are some of the advantages and disadvantages? They may not cause pollution but they are expensive to install and take up a lot of land space. Could they be placed at sea?

CHAPTER VII

THE THREAT TO THE LIVING WORLD

Children will know that warmth and light come from the sun, but do they realise that the sun is the source of our energy? What do they think energy is? Where do they get their energy from? When do they use it? What about plants and animals? Do they get their energy in the same way? Children need to know about the process of photosynthesis in order to understand the role of energy from the sun within the food chain.

FOOD CHAINS

Photosynthesis, the process by which plants convert carbon dioxide and nutrients to carbohydrates, using energy from sunlight, is not an easy concept for children to understand. It is important for them to learn that only plants can take energy directly from the sun, and that any energy passed on to the next consumer is taken from the plant or creature being eaten. Once they grasp the idea that everything in nature is part of a constant cycle, they will be able to work out food chains for themselves. When they have had a lot of practice in relating the wildlife they have been studying to food chains, they will be ready to understand that poisons, as well as nutrients, can be passed through the consumers and accumulate the further up the chain they go, so that creatures near to or at the top can be badly affected, for example, otters and peregrines.

Food Factories: All the children decide what plants they want to be. They take some yellow powder paint,

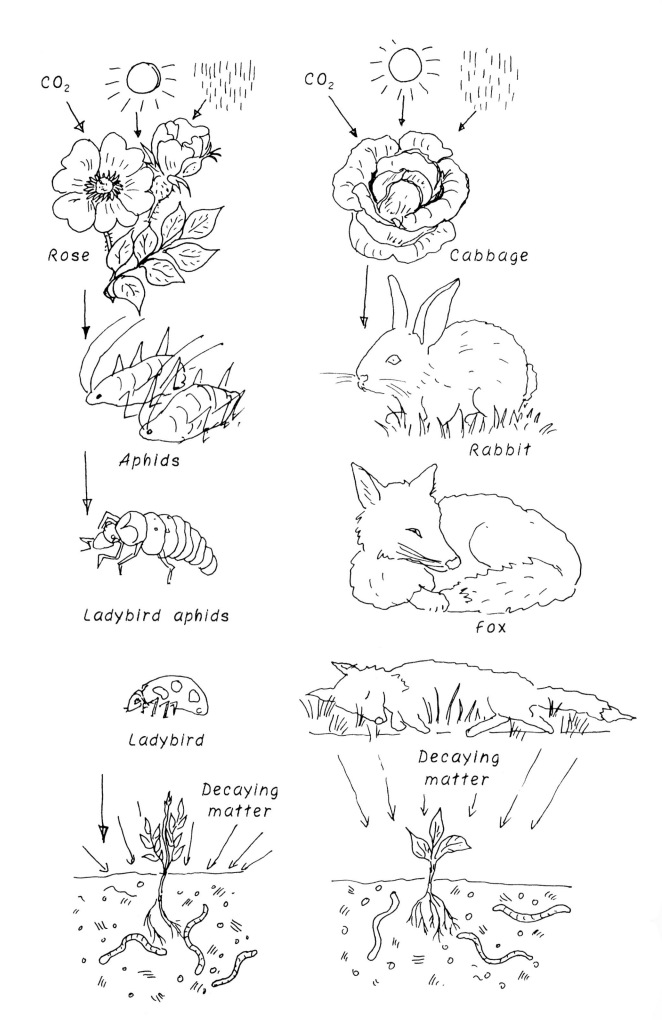

CO_2

Rose

Aphids

Ladybird aphids

Ladybird

Decaying
matter

CO_2

Cabbage

Rabbit

fox

Decaying
matter

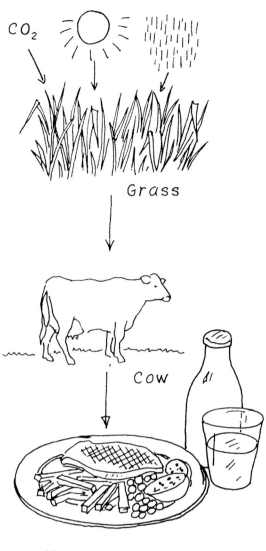

Grass

Cow

Human consumption

Decaying matter

representing energy from sunlight, and then dip a straw firmly into some white paint and blow it very gently on to the yellow. This represents the carbon dioxide from the air, and from their breath when they breathe out. What else does their plant need besides sunlight and air? They can take a small jar of water and mix in it some strong blue powder paint; this represents the nutrients brought up from the soil by the water. They mix all the "ingredients" together and make green chlorophyll in a special process called photosynthesis. They can then paint a mural of green plants, using their "chlorophyll". Older children could have planned beforehand to all be plants from the same habitat: for example a deciduous woodland. Can the children think of any plants which don't seem to do this? Where do mushrooms get their food from?

Energy Chain: Each child has a label with the picture and name of a plant or animal (they could be chosen so that everyone is in a food chain). One child, the sun, gives a small yellow streamer to all of the plants, but none to the animals. The plants should already have been given pieces of white, blue and green crepe streamers. They get on with their work making food, giving a puff to the white streamer (carbon dioxide), twisting the yellow (sun) and blue (nutrients) ones together and wrapping them tightly with the green. Then they put the little green packet in their pockets or fasten them to their fronts with a pin.

Now the herbivores come to look for them: rabbits look for cabbage, cows for grass, greenflies for a rose bush, a tadpole for pondweed, etc. The herbivores put their hands on the plants' shoulders or around their waists. Then it is the turn of the carnivores: the fox finds the rabbit, the child finds the cow, the ladybird finds the greenfly and the fish finds the tadpole, etc. They join up with their hands on the herbivores' shoulders or round their waists.

Now, one group at a time, they stick their drawings on a large noticeboard, headed, "Food Chains", making a complete cycle for each ecosystem as illustrated. The final stage is death, then new plants spring up from the nutritious decaying matter to start the new cycle of foodmaking. This is the most simplified model; more detail can be added as children start to appreciate that many animals eat a great variety of foodstuffs and many eat a mixture of both plant and animal life. They will understand that there is not always enough to go round and so there can be great competition for food.

How do we use energy? What does "energetic" mean? If you use up your energy, how do you get some more?

Poison Chain: This activity is based on the "Energy Chain", but this time some poison is added to the "food" streamers in the form of a small piece of red wool. The plants begin to wilt after making their food, the herbivores become tired and lethargic when they eat the plants, but it's the carnivores at the top of the food chain who fall really ill. They have eaten the poisoned plant and the poisoned animal.

Chain Gangs: Prepare sets of four cards, showing four members of a food chain; each set should be the same colour. The child has to take a card, find the other three members of its food chain, and then put them into the right order.

Food Chain Puzzles: Give a food chain box to a group of three children and ask them to put the pictures in the right order. Each box should contain three pictures: one of a plant, one of a herbivore and one of a carnivore. Older children can have a more complicated food chain to sort out.

Chain Tag: This is a simple tag game with a predator as a chaser; when prey is caught, by being gently touched on the arm, they join the chasers. Some ideas are: lions and gazelles (as lions often hunt in groups there could be several chasers); fox and hens, frogs and herons, frogs and damsel flies, bats and moths, owls and voles. What will happen if the herons eat most of the frogs? Or when the frogs eat a lot of damsel flies?

HABITATS

All living things have a place where they live which is their home. People use their intelligence and skills to adapt their surroundings - their buildings, clothing - and this enables them to live in all sorts of places. We can find animals and plants in all sorts of places too, but each is specially adapted to its own habitat and the conditions in which it lives. Consequently, should something happen to the habitat or the conditions change, the plant or animal will be affected. This in turn will affect the whole balance of the ecosystem, as all living things are interdependent and one change will trigger off a whole sequence of related effects.

Homes: Discuss the concept of "home" with the children, using the following questions. What is your home like? How do you keep warm? How do you get food? Water? Have you ever moved house? How are you specially adapted to your habitat in winter? In summer? What would you do if your house was flooded or burnt down?

Animals' Homes: Discuss the sorts of homes animals have - holes, nests, in trees, on grass. What is their habitat like? How do they keep warm? Cool? How do they get water? Food? What would they do if their home was destroyed?

Humans' and Animals' Habitats: What are some of the differences between the children's homes and the animals'? How do they both keep warm? Cool? Get food? Water?

Animals Adapting: Together think of ways in which animals have had to change because their habitat has changed, eg Arctic animals become camouflaged in winter against the snow (natural change); foxes living in towns scavage in rubbish bins; water birds like flamingoes or herons find a new area of wetland when theirs dries up (forced change).

CAMOUFLAGE

Spot the Objects: Choose twelve objects of different sizes and colours and hide them in a small area outdoors, so that they are camouflaged against a similar background. Then let pairs of children see how many they can spot, making a note of them or a quick sketch. When they reassemble, they can pool their discoveries and if some are missing, go and look for them again. They could also be divided into two groups, one taking it in turns to hide the objects they have chosen and the other spotting the camouflage. Try to include some litter, such as tins, plastic bags or ice cream wrappers.

After the activity, discuss why some plants and animals use camouflage and why others don't need to (ladybirds, kingfishers). Brainstorm all of the animals you can think of that use some camouflage: deer, zebras, butterflies, chameleons, stick insects. What camouflage would the children use if they wanted to observe wildlife in a wood? Do people use camouflage?

Hidden Animals: Can they paint a "hidden animals" picture by drawing animals camouflaged against the background of their habitat. It could be a rainforest, the savannah or the Arctic snow, for example.

Homes for Animals: Children could make miniature models of a variety of animals' homes in a large tray. Some ides are: a tiny robin's nest in a box; holes of varying dimensions for rabbits and foxes; a badger's sett, a squirrel's drey in a "tree" made of a twig; an otter's holt in a hollow tree on a river bank. Model animals could be made, too.

Names of Animals' Homes: Can they fit the names of the homes to their owners? Den, sty, sett, stable, lair, kennel, drey, web. Which belong to wild animals and which to domestic animals? What other examples can they find?

Animals' Habitats: Get the children to cut out a picture of an animal from a magazine and say where it lives. Can they cut out a suitable habitat for it? Ask them to say one thing about the animal that makes it suitable to live there: for example, a duck has webbed feet to help it swim; a polar bear has thick fur to keep out the cold; otters have two layers of fur to protect them from catching cold in the water. What do the children have to protect them from the cold?

Habitat Advertisements: Every creature needs a particular environment and this is a game to familiarise children with the habitat that each one needs. Have a series of cards with advertisements written on them: for example, "Wanted: a quiet, sunny pond with plenty of dragon-flies and a sloping bank". "Wanted: a wood with plenty of rabbits in the nearby fields and, if possible, free range chickens. Non-hunting area preferred".

Children will soon be able to make up their own advertisements. They could be made into a pack of twin cards: one with the name or picture of the animal, and the other the advertisement. This could be played like pelmanism. (See page 75.)

Woodlands and Cold Forests Britain was once largely forested, but the trees have been continually cleared for farming and building, transforming the landscape. Some of the few forest areas that remain are remnants of the royal hunting grounds, like the New Forest. As trees are felled, the native forests are more likely to be replaced by monoculture pine forests, which have little wildlife and are more vulnerable to insect attack as there is no longer a balanced ecosystem.

Deciduous and Evergreen Trees: Go for a "tree walk" and identify the deciduous trees and the evergreens. Older children could make sketches of both kinds. When would it be easiest to do this exercise? Are there some trees or bushes of each kind in the school grounds or garden? Collect fallen leaves from the ground in autumn; can the children sort them into deciduous and evergreen? Are evergreen leaves always green? What is the main difference between the two groups? Is it shape, size or texture? Why are the evergreen leaves thick and shiny or spiked? Take two transparent plastic food bags and attach one to a deciduous tree twig with its leaves and the other to an evergreen branch. Leave them there for a day and then gently unfasten the bags. What do they find? Was there a difference between the two? Now take a bare twig from a deciduous tree and an evergreen twig and repeat the experiment. Why do the deciduous trees need to shed their leaves in winter?

Tell the Age of a Conifer: If you count the number of rings on a pine tree (where branches grow round the same spot on the trunk), it will tell you how old

it is: it produces one new swirl each year. (Try this on your Christmas tree - not if it's plastic!)

Cones: Let the children gather cones from under the various confier trees then sort and label them. What are the differences between them?

Open and Closed Cones: Put some cones, open and closed, in two separate plastic bags, one with a little water in and the other with no water. Place the wet bag in a damp place and the dry one in a warm dry spot. What happens? Why is this? Look at the seeds: how will they get away from the tree and what kind of weather is best?

A Fallen Tree: If it is possible to arrange a visit to a fallen tree, it is well worth it; it may be one that has been blown down or logged. The children could find out why it has fallen. Was it because of a gale? Was it diseased? Was it chopped down for wood to use or because there was not enough space for every tree to grow properly? They can explore the lichen, moss and fungi that may have started to invade it. Have any mini-beasts made their homes there? (See page 37.) What will happen to the tree? Will most of it be carted away, if this has not happened already? What about the roots? What would happen to the tree if it was left there? Would it rot away? What helps it to rot? (Children must wear gloves if they want to take samples).

Role Play: Cutting Down Your Tree: The class have adopted their own tree; they have visited it regularly throughout the seasons; they have rubbed its bark and made pictures of it. (See page 36.) Now

they have to imagine that it is going to be cut down. Working in small groups they could think of reasons why it should stay alive: they play around it, it gives them shade from the sun, it's been growing for a long time. Other groups could be the wood- cutters and think of reasons why it has to go: to make furniture, it is too crowded, it is too old, it may be diseased. What could the children do if the wood-cutters still want to cut it down? Explain that people in many parts of the world are faced with this situation.

AREAS UNDER THREAT: REGIONAL CASE STUDIES

THE PLAINS REGION

The main problems in plains regions relate to the destruction of habitat and conflict of use. In the United States and the steppelands of Asia the plains have now been largely converted to monoculture - the grasslands are huge wheat prairies. This has posed serious problems for species which used to live on the plains; moreover, the monocultures are more vulnerable to disease and attack by insects and by the weather conditions. Native animals, like the bison, were decimated by the new settlers in their thousands. But even if they had been spared, they could not have survived the destruction of their habitat. Now only a few remain in special reserves.

The plains of Africa have been increasingly taken over by domestic herds and cultivation so that nomadic species and tribes have less and less land where they can travel freely. Fertile land is much more scarce due to overgrazing and cultivation which, together with lack of rainfall, lead to erosion of the soil and desertification. The wildlife of the savannah cannot adapt to the harsh conditions of the desert, so they either perish or compete in the diminishing areas that are still available to them. People, too, find it difficult to live in these areas plagued by famine, and often need to change their whole way of life.

Animals in the Savannah: The children can make a list of animals that live in the savannah and collect pictures of them. Can they tell how each one is adapted to its environment?

The Masai: They can find out about the lives of the people of the Masai tribe from films and books.

Making a Model of the Savannah: Let them make a model of the savannah on a large tray with dried out turf and sand, and twigs for trees. One end could be partially sandy, with sparse vegetation. Small model animals could be made from clay or card: wildebeasts, lions, elephants. A herd of cattle could graze on what grass there is. When there is no more grass for them to eat, what can their owners, the Masai, do to keep them alive? Why do the Masai need their cattle?

Project on Native Americans: This would be a good introduction to an understanding of how outsiders can invade and conquer new lands, interfering with whole habitats and the lives of indigenous peoples. Children can be told of the words of Chief Seattle: "This we know. The Earth does not belong to man. Man belongs to the Earth". Help them to understand the relationship that the native Americans had with nature, for example, how they were careful not to kill more bison than they needed for food and clothing, even saying a prayer before hunting to make sure that they would not be greedy and kill too many. There are a number of books and slide packs which give true accounts of what happened to the native North Americans and these will help to counteract the stereotypes that children still have of cowboys and Indians. An excellent example is: "Unlearning Indian Stereotypes" by the Council for Interracial Books for Children, 1841 Broadway, New York.

Native American Name Game: This is for older children once they have learnt something of the culture of the native Americans. Each one chooses a name from nature, rather like the American Indians used to do: for example, "Laughing Water", "Blue Smoke", "Sitting Bull". This requires quite a bit of ingenuity, so the class could pool ideas if they run short. Alternatively, younger children could use their own local environment as the source of their name.

When each one has chosen a nature name, they say their name in turn and give an appropriate hand symbol. Then they go round again giving only their symbol. Now they are able to communicate in silence.

THE TROPICAL RAINFORESTS

Tropical rainforests are being destroyed at the rate of 10 million hectares a year - an area greater than the size of Britain. Forests have been cleared for cattle ranching and large scale agriculture. The rural poor and settlers from overcrowded cities also clear forest areas for their subsistence. None of these practices are viable in the long term, owing to the poor soil. Thus, more and more land is cleared. In addition, cash crops to pay international debts and logging for timber to wealthier countries amounts to 60 million cubic metres exported annually.

Yet rainforests are of great importance. They contain at least half of all the species on Earth and it is estimated that ten percent of these could become extinct by the year 2,000. Many of the foodstuffs and medicines originate in the rainforests: cocoa, citrus, fruits, spices and quinine. Many species are being destroyed before their value is discovered and many creatures, whose habitat is the rainforest, are at risk; for example, the orang-utan, the giant otter, the woolly spider monkey, the golden lion tamarin and lowland and mountain gorillas, to name but a few. Plants are threatened, too - the African violet and the Honduras mahogany. The destruction of the rainforests also has a major impact on climatic conditions.

Native peoples like the Penan of Sarawak in Malaysia, the Chacobo Indians of Bolivia and the Yanomami in the Amazon are being deprived of their very existence by the introduction of Western diseases, by attacks with firearms and by the destruction of their habitat. In this century, 90 Indian tribes have been destroyed in Brazil. Their knowledge of sustainable forestry and of the use of plants is irreplaceable.

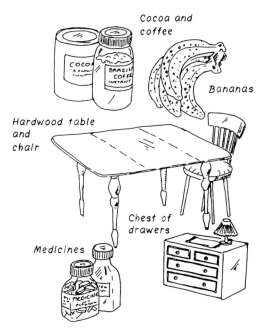

Cocoa and coffee

Bananas

Hardwood table and chair

Chest of drawers

Medicines

Goods from the Rainforest: The children could find out which typical household objects may have come from the rainforests. For example, many foodstuffs in the kitchen, like bananas, cocoa, coffee; a hardwood mahogany table in the living room; medicines in the bathroom; wooden chests of drawers in the bedrooms.

A Rainforest Shop: Do the children know where the food that they eat comes from? Can they find out by collecting empty packets and tins. Although the foodstuffs may now be cultivated elsewhere, many of their favourite foods had their origin in the tropical rainforests. The class shop can sell cocoa; coffee; citrus fruits like oranges, grapefruits, lemons, limes, tangerines; exotic fruits such as mango and papaya, bananas, kumquats and pineapples; spices like cinnamon, cloves, pepper, nutmeg and vanilla; nuts like brazils and cashews; and vegetables like yams and sweet potato. They may be able to find out about new species, for example, some supermarkets are promoting a cross between the grapefruit and the pomelo, which is a green grapefruit. It could be a good idea to have a special promotion of the brazil nut, which still grows in quantity in the tropical forests and which would provide a valuable source of export. Original wild species do not have the same diseases as ones cultivated elsewhere, so what would happen if we lost the original native plants? Some of the more exotic foods are expensive, so children can make models to display in their shop, based on pictures they have seen.

Model Rainforest: Children can make their own rainforest trees with cardboard and paper, packed close together to make the thick canopy of the high trees, the aerial roots and the ferns and creepers. Alternatively, they can make one big tree and hang on cut-outs of monkeys, macaws, blue morpho butterflies and red-eyed frogs. They can display pictures of any of the wildlife of the tropical forests, and videos and slides can give them a picture of the immense wealth of colours and luxuriant vegetation.

Furniture Models: What is furniture generally made of? Do they know which wood might come from the rainforests? Which comes from temperate forests? They could make models of furniture out of card or balsa wood and glue. Paint one set from the rainforests dark brown, varnish it and label the wood. Make another set but keep it natural or painted light brown to represent wood from the temperate forests and label it: oak, ash, maple, etc. These pieces of furniture can be used in a simple doll's house made from cardboard boxes, or in a model of a school room.

Furniture Shop Role Play: The furniture could then be sold in a "shop". People who want a dark colour, but do not want to have rainforest trees, ask for their furniture to be stained a dark brown. Some customers might not know or care about the logging of the rainforests and another one might tell them what was happening. Older children might write to local timber merchants to find out where the wood that they sell comes from, or organise a poster campaign to ask people not to buy hard wood from the rainforests.

CHAPTER VIII
THREATENED SPECIES

By studying a small selection of species under threat, children will get a more in-depth picture of the nature of their plight and be able to draw parallels with other threatened species. The creatures chosen all have a special appeal for young children: parrots, elephants, whales, dolphins and otters. They could equally well concentrate on pandas, gorillas, the black lion tamarin, the woolly spider monkey, the Mediterranean monk seal, the Orinoco crocodile or Queen Alexandra's birdwing butterfly (the world's largest and most threatened butterfly). These creatures are all under threat and more details can be obtained from many of the conservation agencies.

SAVE OUR SPECIES CAMPAIGN

The children can organise a campaign with posters, banners and badges to raise awareness of a threatened animal. They might: send for literature from campaigning organisations; make a radio programme, giving information about why the animal is under threat and what people can do about it; invite an audience to the launch of their campaign

Extinction is Forever: Dinosaurs is a popular topic with most young children and offers a way of introducing the idea of the threat to today's species.

How do scientists think the dinosaurs became extinct? This could lead to a discussion of the ways in which all creatures are adapted to their habitats. (See page 86.)

The main aim at this stage is to foster a deep appreciation of all living things, which will form the basis of protecting and caring for them. The children should already have had plenty of experience of looking after plants and small creatures in school and their immediate environment and can now extend their interests to wider areas.

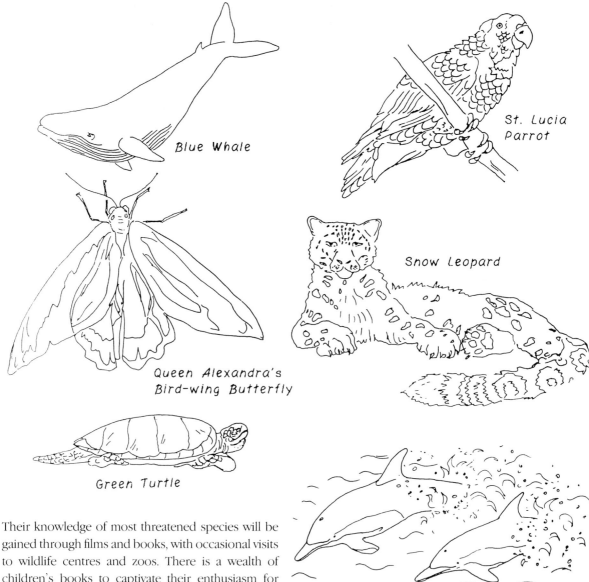

Blue Whale

St. Lucia Parrot

Snow Leopard

Queen Alexandra's Bird-wing Butterfly

Green Turtle

Dolphins

Their knowledge of most threatened species will be gained through films and books, with occasional visits to wildlife centres and zoos. There is a wealth of children's books to captivate their enthusiasm for wild animals, for example.

There are some excellent nature programmes on television and many teachers are now taping them to show them to their classes, choosing appropriate clips from such series as Nature, Life on Earth and Disappearing World. Films and videos are also available from organisations such as the National Geographical Society and the Royal Society for the Protection of Birds. (See list of useful organisations on page 86.)

ANIMALS – DOMESTIC AND WILD

Pets: Many families have pets and children could make a list of which pets they have at home and make a pictogram of them. (Teachers should use their discretion if this is a sensitive area. If some pupils are not allowed to have pets, then look at pets that children like best.) Some children might be able to

bring their pet to school, with their parents' co-operation, and talk about how they look after it.

Are all pets well looked after? Why are there so many stray dogs and cats? A visiting speaker from the RSPCA could be invited to talk to older children, as long as they emphasised the caring aspect. (The film "Kes" is a good illustration of the bond that can develop between children and their pets.)

Exercise for Dogs: Where can the children let their dog have a good run? Dogs need to be safe from traffic and people need to be protected from dog excrement. How can people train their dogs not to soil the pavements or public places? Children should know of the dangers of touching dog excrement, even by accident. This is why they should always wear gloves when touching soil.

After thinking about the needs of their pets, children can go on to consider the situation of wild animals in captivity. They can make categories of domestic and wild animals.

A Visit to the Zoo: If a visit to a zoo is possible, a discussion about keeping animals in zoos could follow. Are there different kinds of zoos, for example, ones where animals have space to roam? What about safari parks? Supposing animals are disappearing in the wild. Is it best to keep some of them safe in zoos?

Class Pets: What about class pets? They have to be kept in cages. Could the class debate whether or not to have a pet? One idea might be to loan a small pet like a gerbil or rabbit from children who have pets at home with enough space for runs. They could be looked after for a week or so and then returned.

Threatened Animals Pelmanism: Make up a number of cards showing various animals under threat, two of each kind with their name underneath. Play in pairs with the cards face downwards on the table. One player turns one card over and then a second one; if they are the same he takes them, if not, he puts them face down in place. Then the second player has a turn, and so on, until all the cards have been paired. Older pupils can draw and colour their own cards and write the name of the animal underneath. After the game they could tell the class anything they know about the animals in their sets and why they are threatened.

Yanomami Children: Ask the children to imagine that they are members of the Yanomami tribe in the Amazon and the trees are being cut down nearer and nearer to their village.

They can discuss how they can use the forest for their needs without destroying it. What would their needs be if they were members of the Yanomami tribe? Could they cut a few trees down, making spaces here and there? How could they be sure that there would still be enough trees to prevent soil erosion and to supply their needs in the future? They could replace some of their model trees ("model rainforest" see page 72) with saplings and other spaces could be used to cultivate maize.

"Hippos Know about the Environment too": This is an imaginative, but topical story of a young girl called Stephanie, who answers an advertisement: "Wanted: friendly homes for hippos". In due course the hippo arrives on her doorstep, to the consternation of her parents. He explains that everything has changed in his waterhole: a motorway has been built nearby; the forests cleared; the land sprayed with chemicals; the rivers dammed. He and all of his other animal friends just had to move. Stephanie's parents say that they are sorry but he cannot possibly stay there and it's really nothing to do with them. The hippo asks if they drink coffee from his country, Tanzania. Do they buy cashew nuts that are grown there, or wear clothes from its cotton? They say they do, and realising that the hippo's "problems" are their's too, he is finally allowed to stay. He turns out to be a big soft toy that Stephanie puts at the top of her bed and uses as a pillow!

This story could be the basis of creative writing by the children or a theme for a role-play. (Ref: Hepworth, T Forum, WCCI Publications 1991.)

THREATENED SPECIES

The African Elephant: African elephants have been disappearing for some time. Between 1970 and 1989, their numbers fell from 2 million to 625,000, showing that urgent steps are needed to prevent them from becoming extinct. Loss of habitat (owing to the increasing demand for land by the growing human population, combined with their slaughter for ivory are the main threats. As they need between 200 and 400 kilograms of plant food each day, the concentration of the elephant communities into small areas causes widespread devastation to the plant life in those areas with drastic effects on the whole ecological system. At last, in 1990, most major industrialised cities agreed to a ban on trade in ivory, although poachers are still successful in tracking down and killing whole elephant communities for their tusks, even penetrating into the reserves which have been set up to give them protection and a habitat which meets their needs.

ELEPHANTS

Making an Elephant: Clay is a good medium for the modelling of an elephant, but children can use cardboard or junk materials. (One way of making an elephant can be found in "Animals to Make". See Bibliography on page 82.)

Elephants in the Savannah: Miniature elephants can be made out of Plasticine, play dough or clay to go in the model of the savannah grasslands.

The Six Blind Men: Read the story in World Studies 8-13 (S Fisher and D Hicks) about the six blind men who all thought that the part of the elephant that they were touching was the whole animal. Discuss what this means. Can people have very different opinions about the same thing? For example, certain animals: spiders, camels, grizzly bears.

Asian and African Elephants: By looking at pictures, can the children find out some of the differences and similarities between Asian and African elephants?

Souvenirs: Ask the children what sort of souvenirs they might bring back from holiday to open a discussion on illegal trade and gifts. Older children could design a poster to discourage people from buying such souvenirs.

PROTECT THE PARROT

One hundred species of parrot - nearly one third of the world's total - are now severely threatened; 77 of them are in immediate danger of extinction. Their beauty and ability to imitate make them the most popular of pet birds. In 1986 alone more than 600,000 parrots were traded between different countries and thousands more are caught and smuggled illegally. It is estimated that half the parrots that are caught die of fright or due to the change of food before they are exported. A lot more suffocate in overcrowded travelling cages or in quarantine; ones that are smuggled are crammed into even smaller cages. So only one in five of the parrots caught in the wild make it alive, to be sold in pet shops.

People who want parrots as pets should make sure that they are bred in captivity in their own country, as in the case for budgerigars and cockatiels. All the parrots people want in Britain can be bred in this country.

The Case of the Spix Macaw: Parrot conservationists say that there is only one Spix Macaw left in the wild. It is a beautiful bright blue parrot, with a very long tail and drooping wings whilst in flight. Have the children any idea how it might be saved? There are fifteen Spix Macaw known to be in captivity and probably many more held in secret - could it be in the bird's habitat in North East Brazil in the woodlands of Caraiba trees? Could conservationists capture the last bird? The class could discuss what could be done. What about the part played by zoos? Could captive bred parrots return to the wild?

Keeping a Budgie: Did your class know that budgies are part of the parrot family? What things does a budgie need to keep it well and happy? The

These diagrams are rough guidelines. Use squared paper to adapt drawings to a larger scale.

MAKE A PARROT

Cut out basic shape on two pieces of card or felt. Stuff with old tights / wool etc. and staple or glue along the black outline. Paint and cut out feathers. Stick on. Stick, sew or staple pipe cleaners for the claws.

children could interview owners to find out why they like to have a budgie as a pet. What is their routine for looking after it?

From the Tropical Forests to Britain: Ask the children to imagine that they are a baby parrot captured from the tropical forests. How were they caught? Was it by someone climbing up to their nest? Did they fly into a net? Were their trees being cut down? What happened when they travelled to Britain? What did it feel like? What was it like in the pet shop? Do they still remember the forest?

Make a Parrot: With the help of illustrations of brightly coloured parrots, children draw an outline on two pieces of card, as shown in the diagram. They then colour them, stick on the wings and stuff them with pieces of old tights and staple them together. Coloured felt can be used in the same way, making a collage of different colours, or crepe paper cut into feathers can be stuck on to the body and wings. Pipe-cleaners can be stuck on as feet and the model bird can be hung as a mobile or stood up with a wedge of Plasticine. A whole mobile of different coloured parrots could brighten up the classroom. (See also "Animals to Make" listed on page 84.)

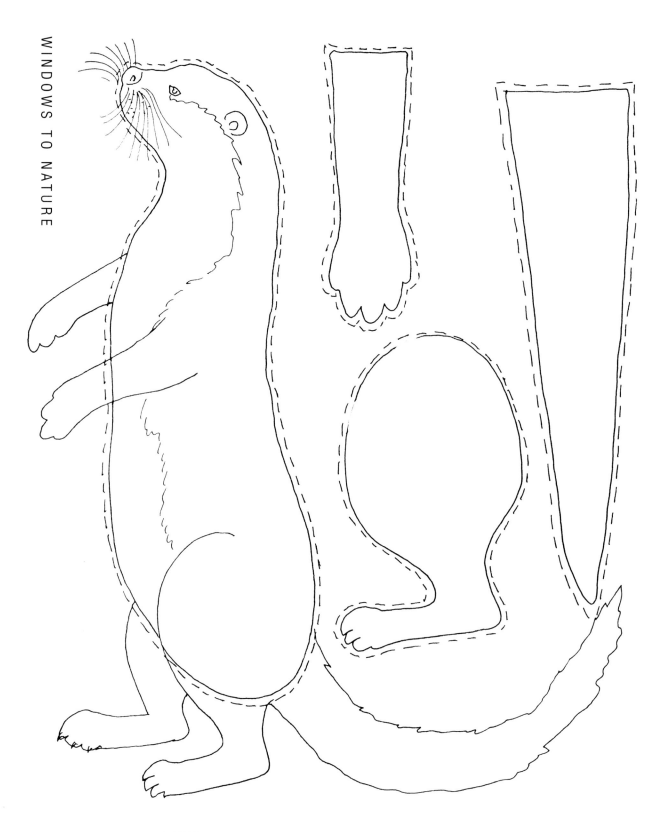

MAKE AN OTTER

Cut out basic shape on two pieces of felt or velvet I inch out from the dotted line to allow for stuffing. Sew or stick them together leaving a space at the base. Turn inside out and fill with stuffing. Cut out, sew and stuff tail, arms and legs (cut ½ inch out from the dotted line to allow for stuffing). Sew onto body. Sew or stick on beads, felt or velvet for eyes. Use velvet or felt for ears and nose. Cotton threads for whiskers. Stick on cream or grey coloured felt or velvet for the underside of the otter. For simpler otters use cut out velvet or felt for the arms, legs and tail and stick on unstuffed.

78

OTTERS

Eurasian otters were once widespread in Britain and the rest of Europe but in the late 1950s and early 1960s they underwent a sudden and catastrophic decline. They have now completely disappeared from the rivers of central and southern England and are now only found in the Souh West and Welsh borders of England; in Wales, Scotland and Ireland there are healthier numbers. There are several reasons for their decline. Farmers draining bogs, streams and rivers, dredging and clearing banks combined with recreation activities such as fishing and boating have led to a loss of habitat.

Pesticides and chemicals from industrial waste may have poisoned the otter's food supply, as they are at the top of the food chain. Polluted water can also lead to disease. Otter hunting with hounds has only recently been completely banned. Trappers also hunted otters for their pelts. In 1978, an order came into effect giving otters complete protection. A number of otters are killed on roads as they try to move to new habitats.

An attempt is now being made to bring otters back to their former haunts by reintroducing captive bred animals to the wild. Otter havens are being established where river banks are being planted and kept free from human disturbance, and artificial holts are being tried out for breeding and shelter during the daytime.

Make an Otter: Cut an outline, as illustrated, from double pieces of brown velvet or fur fabric. Sew or stick them together leaving a space underneath and fill it with stuffing. Cut out webbed feet and glue them on. The eyes, nose and ears can be pieces of black velvet stuck on. Younger children could cut out just one thickness of the outline and stick it on the display board, drawing in its whiskers.

Model an Otter: Make clay or Plasticine models of otters, emphasising their streamlined bodies. Some models could be on all fours, others could sit upright.

Otters' Habitats: The children can look at photos and pictures of otters. How are they specially adapted to their habitat? They have a thick waterproof coat, streamlined body, and webbed feet. Get the children to find out as much as they can about otters.

Food Chains: How many food chains can they make with an otter at the top? For example, small aquatic plants · damsel flies · frogs · otters; or duckweed · minnows · eels · otters. Younger children could be more general: water plants · insects · small fish · eels · otters. This is a follow-up to work on food chains.

Tarka the Otter: Show the film of Tarka the Otter and read some excerpts from the book. The children could act out some of the sequences they like best.

Tarkina the Otter: Tell the story of the baby otter, orphaned and injured by a terrier on the Isle of Skye, who was nursed back to health and became a film star at the age of three months as the baby in Tarka the Otter. This true story was shown on Clapperboard, and Mike Rosenberg has made a film of her rescue. A book describing this adventure is "Tarkina the Otter" by John Goldsmith, Pelham Books, 1981.

Protecting the Otter: The children can find out about the Otters and Rivers Project from the Royal Society for Nature Conservation. How are they planning to get captive otters back into the wild? Why is it so difficult? Some wildlife parks keep otters, or you can telephone the Otter Trust, Bungay, Nr Lowestoft to arrange a visit. (Tel 0986 893470.).

Otters' Holts: Can the children think what otters would need for their homes? (Easy access to rivers. They need to be warm and dry. A tunnel burrowed from the water to a dry area. A holt lined with grass and reeds for bedding.)

WHALES AND DOLPHINS

There are two types of whale: the baleen whale and the toothed whale.

The Baleen Whale has a food filtering device to sieve minute organisms like krill, also crustacae and small fish. They include the blue whale and the humpback whale, also the minke whale, which has been sighted off Britain's shores.

The Toothed Whales include the killer and pilot whales, both of which have been recorded in the seas round Britain. The sperm whale features in the story of Moby Dick and excerpts of this could be read to the children to give a good idea of the immense power of these creatures. Toothed whales use a type of sonar as echo location to help them in navigation and the detection of prey, crustaceans and fish. Whales, like dolphins, are gentle, playful creatures which exhibit co-operative behaviour, such as caring for the sick or wounded; they have been seen to help a fellow whale get to the surface to breathe.

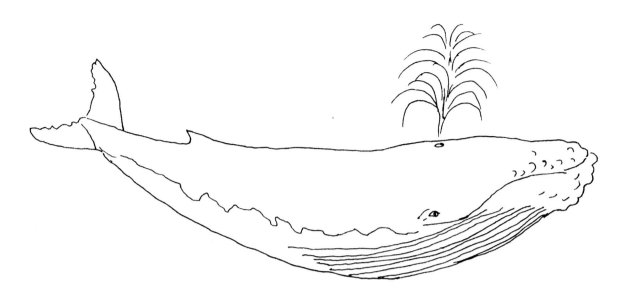

Whales are threatened by commercial whalery for meat and oil, which has exploited almost every whale species. It is now partly controlled by the International Whaling Commission, with 41 nations represented; but the Commission has no real powers of enforcement. Some countries, notably Japan, have taken advantage of the loophole which allows whales to be caught for "scientifc research', which means that a lot of killing still goes on. Many organisations have fought long and hard to achieve the whaling moritorium and are continuing to endeavour to enforce it.

How much bigger is a whale than an elephant? The quoted number is 30 elephants, but children can work it out for themselves. A whale can weigh up to 130,000 kg and can reach over 25 m in length - about as long as three railway carriages! Visit the Natural History Museum in London to get a real idea of the size of the blue whale.

Whale Music: Play a tape of the humpback whale and let the children make up a dance to its sound.

Dolphins: Harmful fishing practices include the development of enormous plastic fishing nets that sweep up all living creatures from the bottom to the top of the ocean, upsetting the breeding balance by depleting the stock of the young. The nets cause death to innumerable creatures that get entangled in them.

Although many sea creatures get caught up in the nets, the story of the dolphin's plight is the most tragic. Yellow fish tuna swim under dolphins, who keep near the surface to be able to breathe. Tuna fishing is an enormous industry now, and when the fishermen cast their nets great quantities of dolphins are caught as well and are either drowned or killed in the process. The outcry in the United States over these killings was so great that many shops announced that they would stop selling fish caught by boats that kill dolphins in their nets and only use fish caught by the traditional line and pole methods. Dolphins are also threatened by pollution, especially near shores where there has been domestic and industrial discharge and sewage dumping. Dolphins are at the head of the food chain so they are particularly vulnerable.

As dolphins use sound for both echolocation and communication, the increase in noise from human activities such as power boats, jet skis and marinas, also the use of sonar echo sounders, greatly affects their hearing systems and they are increasingly moving away from human habitation. The common and the bottlenose have been the most frequently reported dolphin species in British waters, but their numbers have greatly declined in recent years.

Make a Dolphin: Cut out two pieces of thin card as illustrated, put stuffing between them and secure it with thin wire. Then cover the whole with papier mache and paint. Stick on flippers. Dolphins modelled in clay can show their streamlined shape.

Dolphin Film: Show a video of dolphins and then let children paint a mural of them, both in and above the sea. Food Chains: Dolphins eat many kinds of fish, including mullet, moray eels, flounder, cod, mackerel and pilchards. The children can make up a food chain or mobile starting from microscopic plants, through small crustaceans, to various sizes of fish. Which is the greater predator of the dolphins?

MAKE A DOLPHIN

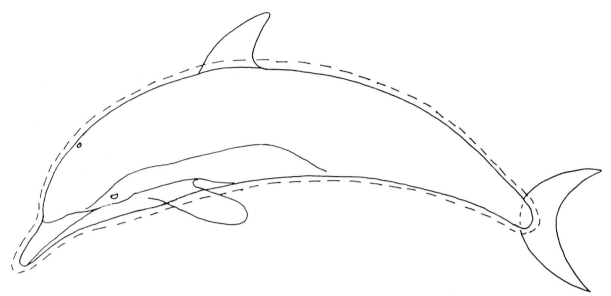

This diagram is a guide only. For a larger stuffed dolphin use squared paper to enlarge or draw freehand.

1. Using pieces of thin card, cut out basic dolphin shape leaving a narrow margin. Place stuffing within the body shape and join the edges of the card with glue or staples.

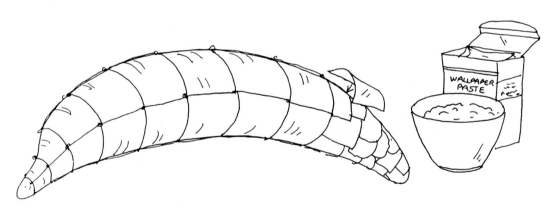

2. Secure with thin wire as shown. Cover the whole with papier mache and paint. Stick on flippers, fins and tail.

Performing Dolphins: Have any of the children seen performing dolphins in a zoo, a leisure park or on television? Do they think the dolphins are happy doing this, or would they be happier in the sea? What about other performing animals: chimpanzees? circus horses? bears? How are they trained? Is it by kindness or cruelty, or a bit of both?

The Dolphin's Touch: This short film, shown on Channel 4's Picture Box, is about a friendly dolphin. It shows people who are depressed, swimming with the dolphin and feeling much better. There are fine underwater shots of the dolphin's movements and the film ends by asking whether dolphins and other marine creatures like to be captive and performing.

BIBILIOGRAPHY AND USEFUL ADDRESSES

Books for Teachers

Barton, M. **Why do People Harm Animals?** Franklin Watts 1988

Birmingham Development Education Centre. **Get the Picture**. BDEC 1989

Birmingham Development Education Centre. **Shared Learning**. BDEC 1989

Birmingham Development Education Centre. **Theme Work: Images, Change, Transport, Tanzania**. BDEC 1986

Birmingham Development Education Centre. **What is a Family?** BDEC 1985

Borba, M and C. **Self Esteem: A Classroom Affair Vols I & II**. Winston Press 1978

BBC. **The Music Box Song Book**. BBC 1987

Bronze, L, Heathcote N and Brown, P. **The Blue Peter Green Book**. BBC Books 1990

Burford, D. **The Magical Earth Secrets**. Western Canadian Wilderness Committee 1990

Caduto, M and Bruchac, J. **Keepers of the Earth. Native Stories and Environmental Activities for Children**, Fifth House Publisher 1989

Centre for World Development Education. **The Primary School for a Changing World**. CWDE 1989

Cornell, J B. **Sharing Nature with Children**. Exley Publications 1979

Cornell, J B. **Sharing the Joy of Nature**. Dawn Publicatons 1989

Cole, J. **Evolution**. A & C Black 1987

Dauncey, G. **Earth Crisis**. Hobsons Publishing 1990

Earthkids Project. The Urban Wildlife Trust 1990

Elkington J and Hailes J. **The Young Green Consumer Guide**. Douglas Hill 1990

Ellis C. **Water**. BBC Fact Finders 1990

Fisher, S and Hicks D. **World Studies 8-13**. Oliver & boyd 1989

Foreman. **One World**. Andersen Press 1990

Fountain, S. **Learning Together**. Stanley Thornes Ltd/WWF 1990

Goldsmith. **Tarkina the Otter**. Pelham Books 1981

Gould League of Victoria. **Environmental Starters**. GLV 1989

Gould League of Victoria. **Environmental Games**. GLV 1989

Gregory, M. **Exploring Indian Crafts**. Mantra Books 1990

Grunsell, A. **Bullying**. Franklin Watts 1990

Hedges, P and Scott, S. **Water**. Birmingham DEC 1990

Hendricks, G and Wills, R. **The Centering Book**. Prentice Hall 1975

Holland, B and Lucas, H. **Caring for Planet Earth**. Lion Publishing 1990

Horton P. **Earth Watch**. BBC Fact Finders 1990

IYSH. **Doorways**. Ikon Productions 1987

Jill's Class. **The Greenhouse Effect**. Hackney Schools Publishing Project 1989

Johnson, G. **How You Can Save the Planet**. Temeron Books 1990

Liebmann, M. **Art Games and Structures for Change**. Croom Helm 1986

Lyle, S and Roberts, M. **An Arctic Child**. Greenlight Publications 1989

Lyle, S and Roberts, M. **A Rainforest Child**. Greenlight Publications 1988

Lyle, S and Roberts, M. **Tomorrow's Woods**. Greenlight Publications 1987

Maindenhead Teachers' Centre. **Doing Things**. Trentham books 1983

Mares, C and Stephenson, R. **Inside, Outside**. Tidy Britain Group

Marsh, L. **Along Came Man**. Piper Publications. WWF 1986

Masheder, M. **Let's Co-operate**. Peace Education Project 1986

Masheder, M. **Let's Play Together**. Green Print 1989

Mattias, B and Thomson, R. **My Body A-Z**. Franklin Watts 1988

McCormick, J. **Acid Rain**. Franklin Watts 1985

Moses, B. **Catching the Light**. WWF 1991

Moses, B and Corbett, P. **The Music Box Song Book**, BBC 1987

Nutkins, T. **Pets**. BBC Fact Finders 1990

Oxfam. **The World in a Supermarket Bag: an Activity on Food**. Oxfam 1987

Oxford Development Education Unit. **Roots and Shoots: A Schools Garden Project**. ODEU 1988

Parker, P. **Water for Life**. Simon & Schuster 1990

Paychett, L. **Clean Air, Dirty Air**. A & C Black 1990

Pollock, S. **Dinosaurs**. BBC Fact Finders 1990

Pollock, S. **Wildlife Safari**. BBC Fact Finders 1990

Potter, T. **Weather**. BBC Fact Finders 1990

Randle, D. (ed) **Green Teacher**, Machynlleth, Powys, Wales, SY2 0BD

Randle, D. **Teaching Green**. Green Print, Merlin Press 1989

Richards, R. **An Early Start to Nature**. Simon & Schuster 1989

Richards, R. **An Early Start to Science**. Simon & Schuster 1987

Richards, R. **An Early Start to Technology from Science**. 1990

Robbins, R. **Looking at Nature**. BBC Books 1989

Rogers, R. **Freedom to Learn**. Charles Merrill 1985

Rose, D. **The People who Hugged the Trees**. Rinehart 1990

Rose, P and Conlon, A. **Yanomamo** (musical). WWF 1983

Rose, P and Conlon, A. **African Jigsaw** (musical). WWF 1986

Rose, P and Conlon, A. **Ocean World** (musical). WWF 1991

Royal Society for Nature Conservation. **Window on Owls Activity Pack**. RSNC 1989

Royal Society for the Protection of Birds. **Action for Birds**. RSPB 1990

Saunders, P. **Feeling Safe**. Franklin Watts 1987

Stevenson, R. **Beating Litter**. Tidy Britain Group 1989

Swallow, S. **The Nature Trail Book of Garden Wildlife**. Usborne 1985

Taylor, B. **Waste and Recycling**. A & C Black 1990

Taylor, B. **Food for Thought**. A & C Black 1990

Taylor, B. **Trees for Tomorrow**. A & C Black 1990

Thomson, R. **Washday**. A & C Black 1990

Thomson, R. **When I was Young**. Early 20th Century History. Franklin Watts 1989

Tidy Britain Group. **Litter, Waste Management and Recycling**. TBG 1988

Tidy Britain Group. **Look Around the Town**. TBG 1989

Tidy Britain Group. **Our Environment**. Nelson 1988

Van Matre, S. **Acclimatisation**. Institute of Earth Education 1972

Van Matre, S et al. **Conceptual Encounters**. Institute of Earth Education 19

Van Matre, S. **Sunship Earth**. Institute of Earth Education 1979

Williams, M., McPherson, T., Mackintosh, M. and Williams, M. **Active Maths**. WWF 1991

Wilson, R. **Starting from a Walk**. Trentham Books 1988

WWF. **Animals to Make**. Scholastic Publications Ltd 1985

WWF. **Focus on Birds. Focus on Flowers. Focus on Insects**. WWF 1990

Book List for Children

Aardema, V. **Bringing the Rain to Kapiti Plain**. Macmillan 1981

Anno, M. **All in a Day**. Hamish Hamilton 1986

Ayres, P. **When Dad Cut Down the Chestnut Tree**. Walker Books 1988

BBC. **Music Time Pupil's Pamphlet**. BBC 1990

BBC. **Science Challenge, Pupil's Book**. BBC/ Longman 1990

Baker, J. **When the Forest Meets the Sea**. Jonathon Cape 1989

Baskerville, J. **Bread. Threads Series**. A & C Black 1987

Bellamy, D. **How Green Are You?** Frances Lincoln 1991

Bjork, C and Anderson, L. **Linnea's Windowsill**. Raben & Sjorgen 1988

Bjork, C and Anderson, L. **Linnea's Almanac**. Raben & Sjorgen 1989

Brown, J. **Where the Forest Meets the Sea**. Walker Books 1987

Burningham, J. **Mr Grump's Motor Car**. Picture Puffin 1979

Burningham, J. **Oi! Get Off Our Train**. Jonathon Cape 1989

Cowcher, H. **Antarctica**. Andre Deutsch 1990

Cowcher, H. **Rainforest**. Andre Deutsch 1988

Davies, K and Oldfield, W. **My Apple**. A & C Black 1990

Davies, K and Oldfield, W. **My Balloon**. A & C Black 1989

Davies, M. and WWF. **My Rare Animal ABC** and **My Rare Animal 123**. WWF 1992

Deshpande, C. **Scrape, Rattle and Blow**. A & C Black 1988

Dixon, A. **Clay**. A & C Black 1989

Dixon, A. **Wool**. A & C Black 1988

Doherty, B. **Spellhorn**. Young Lions Collins 1990

Early Novel. **Fruit Salad. Mixed Vegetables**. Hamish Hamilton 1986

Early Novel. **Vegetables. Tasty Fruit**. Early Novel 1988

Foreman, M. **Dinosaurs and all that Rubbish**. Puffin Books 1974

Foreman, M. **Moose**. Picture Puffin 1973

Foreman, M. **Trick and Tracker**. Gollancz 1981

Foster, J. **A Very First Poetry Book and A First Poetry Book**. OUP 198

Gore, S. My Shadow. **Simple Science Series**. A & C Black 1989

Gnfalconi, A. **Osa's Pride**. Littlebrown 1990

Hamley, D. **Hare's Choice**. Young Lions Collins 1990

Harper, A and Roche, C. **How We Feel**. Kestral Books 1979

Humphrey, M. **The River that Gave Gifts**. Children's Book Press 1987

Jackman, W. **Taste. Hearing. Sight. Touch. Smell**. Wayland 1989

James, S. **Sally and the Limpet**. Walker Books 1991

Keeping, C. **Adam and Paradise Island**. OUP 1989

Ker-Wilson, B. **The Turtle and the Island**. Frances Lincoln 1990

King-Smith, D. **Sophie's Snail**. Walker Books 1989

Leaf, M. **The Story of Ferdinand**. Puffin 1982

Lesikin, J. **Down the Road. A Turtle and a Snake Look for a Home Together**. Prentice Hall 1978

Lewin, H and Kopper, L. **A Flower in the Forest**. Hamish Hamilton 1989

Lewin, H and Kopper, L. **A Shell on the Beach**. Hamish Hamilton 1989

Lionni, L. **It's mine**. Anderson Press 1986

Lionni, L. **Swimmy**. Abelard 1975

Lobel, A. **Frog and Toad Together**. I can read books. Worlds Work 19

Martinez, C (Ed). **Once Upon a Planet**. Puffin 1989

Marzollo, J. **What Else Can You Do?** Bodley Head 1990

Mathieson, F. **Purnima's Parrot**. Magi Publications 1988

McClintock, M. **A Fly Went By**. Collins 1961

McCaffrey, J. **The Swamp Witch**. Bantam 1984

McKee, D. **Tusk Tusk**. Anderson Press 1978

Mendoza, G. **House by Mouse**. Andre Deutsch 1982

Multi-cultural Support Service, Walsall. **The Mice and the Elephant** 1982

Namjoshi, S. **Aditi and the One-eyed Monkey**. Sheba 1986

Oakley, G. **Hetty and Harriet**. Macmillan 1981

Peet, B. **The Wump World**. Andre Deutsch 1976

Pirotta, S. **Do you Believe in Magic?** Dent 1990

Pollock, S and Wingham, P. **Forests in Danger**. Belitha Press 1990

Roth, S. **The Story of Light**. Morrow Junior Books 1990

Scholastic. **Animals to Make**. Scholastic Publications Limited/WWF 1988

Scott, H. **The Plant That Ate the World**. Faber 1989

Seuss, Dr. **The Sneeches and Other Stories**. Collins 1961

Sheldon, D and Blythe, G. **The Whales' Song**. Hutchinson 1990

Silverstein, S. **The Giving Tree**. Jonathon Cape 1987

Snape, J and C. **Giant**. Walker Books 1989

Stone, H. **The Last Free Bird**. Prentice Hall 1967

Vennings, T. **Rocks. Beans**. A & C Black 1990

Vincent, C. **Ernest and Celestine. A Series**. Julia McCrae 1982

Vyner, S. and Vyner, T. **The Stolen Egg**. Victor Gollancz Ltd. WWF 1991

Walpole, B. **Water. Threads Series**. A & C Black 1988

Useful Organisations

Watch: Watch is the junior section of the Royal Society for Nature Conservation and its associated Wildlife Trusts. Watch gets children actively involved in their environment by helping them to understand their surroundings, contribute to scientific research and develop an awareness of the environment. Schools can belong as affiliated members: for £15 a year you get multiple copies of Watchword (the club magazine), LINK and a free copy of the leaders' pack. Watch is planning to expand its services to include more schools packs, links with the National Curriculum requirements and also pre-school and youth group projects. Watch has already carried out the following activities:

"Acid": an award-winning survey of rainfall acidity, undertaken by 20,000 children around the UK; "Ladybird Spot": a survey of Britain's ladybirds which led to the discovery of a species of a two-spotted ladybird thought to be extinct; "Battitudes": the first ever national survey into people's attitudes towards bats; and "Watch on Streams": an opportunity to monitor stream pollution at a local level, using a specially developed "slide rule". There have also been activities on recycling, barn owl surveys, bumblebee walks and there are projects planned on monitoring low-level ozone, surveying dragonflies and investigating tropical forest products in the home. Badges are given for the following observation of wildlife: a project which you have done yourself; nature craft work; practical conservation work, individually or in a group; investigation of part of your environment; keeping a protective eye on your environment; telling people about the environment and what they can do to help. This is an ideal way of getting children to feel that they are part of a movement that will really help to improve the environment and teachers can adapt the many activities to suit the age group that they teach.

Useful Organisations: The Royal Society for the Protection of Birds has a large video and film library of excellent quality, and many of the films and videos can be hired or bought from: The Lodge, Sandy, Bedfordshire, SG19 2DL.

They have attractive posters including a most beautiful one of a kingfisher, and they have produced a booklet on environmental games, some of which are well suited to the younger age group. The Earth Kids Project sets out to provide guides to good practice in the provision of environmental play opportunities for children of pre-school age to age eleven. It produces guides to promote the concepts and benefits of environmentally based play and it lists suitable schemes that young children can participate in every region of the country. The National Association for Environmental Education The NAEE has a lively twice yearly magazine with many practical ideas and has a number of inexpensive practical guides on such subjects as "Organisation of an Out of School Visit and Outdoor Studies"; "An Aquarium in School"; "Using Maps 5-3"; "Developing a School Nature Reserve"; "Creating and Maintaining a Garden to Attract Butterflies"; and many others. West Midlands College of HE, Gorway Walsall, WS1 3BD.

A SELECTION OF ENVIRONMENTAL ORGANISATIONS IN BRITAIN

The following organisations can be useful to teachers.

ACID RAIN INFORMATION CENTRE
Dept of Environmental & Geographical Studies
Manchester Polytechnic
Chester Street
Manchester
M1 5GD
Tel: 061 228 6171 ext 2421
National centre for research, education and information on acid rain

BRITISH BUTTERFLY CONSERVATION SOCIETY
Tudor House, Quorn
Loughborough
Leicestershire, LE12 8AD
Te;: 0509 412870
Promotes conservation of British butterflies.

BRITISH HEDGEHOG PRESERVATION SOCIETY
Knowbury House
Knowbury, Shropshire
Hedgehog research/conservation

BRITISH NATURALISTS' ASSOCIATION
48 Russell Way
Higham Ferrers
Northants NN9 8EJ
Tel: 0245 420756
British natural history. Has youth section

COUNTRYSIDE COUNCIL FOR WALES
Plas Penrhos
Ffordd Penrhos
Bangor
Gwyneth LL57 2LQ
Tel: 0248 37044
Welsh division of the disbanded Nature Conservancy Council. Established to be responsible for the conservation of flora and fauna in Wales

ENGLISH NATURE
Northminster House
Peterborough PE1 1UA
Tel: 0733 340345
English division of the disbanded Nature Conservancy Council. Established to be responsible for the conservation of flora and fauna in England

THE FLORA AND FLORA PRESERVATION SOCIETY
8-12 Camden High Street
London NW1 0JH
Tel: 071 387 9656
International conservation of wild animals and plants, particularly threatened species

FRIENDS OF THE EARTH
26-28 Underwood Road
London N1 7JQ
Energy, transport, countryside conservation, waste recycling, pollution. Produces study packs, posters, resource sheets

GREENPEACE
Greenpeace House
Canonbury Villas
London N1 2PN
Tel: 071 354 5100
Direct action conservationists involved in obstructing whaling, seal culling, dumping of radioactive waste

INTERNATIONAL COUNCIL FOR BIRD
PRESERVATION
32 Cambridge road
Girton
Cambridge CB3 0PJ
Tel: 0223 277318
Determines the status of bird species and their habitats worldwide. Compiles data on endangered species

INTERNATIONAL FUND FOR ANIMAL WELFARE
(IFAW)
Tubwell House
New Road
Crowborough
East Sussex TN6 2QH
Tel: 0892 663374
Campaigns against killing of seals, whales, polar bears, vicuna

INTERNATIONAL SOCIETY FOR THE PREVENTION
OF WATER POLLUTION
Little Orchard
Bentworth
Alton
Hampshire GU34 5RB
Tel: 0420 6225
Aims to prevent water pollution worldwide, to promote research and to disseminate information

JERSEY WILDLIFE PRESERVATION TRUST
Les Augres Manor
Trinity
Jersey
Channel Islands
Tel: 0534 61949
Aims to build up breeding colonies of species threatened with extinction in the wild. Junior Section

MAMMAL SOCIETY
Dexter House
2 Royal Mint Court
London EC3N 4XX
Tel: 071 265 0808
Promotes interest in the study of mammals

MARINE CONSERVATION SOCIETY
9 Gloucester Road
Ross-on-Wye
Herefordshire HR9 5BU
Tel: 0989 66017
Marine conservation

NATURE CONSERVANCY COUNCIL FOR SCOTLAND
12 Hope Terrace
Edinburgh EH9 2AS
Tel: 031 447 4784
Scottish division of the disbanded Nature Conservancy Council. Established to be responsible for the conservation of flora an fauna in Scotland.

MEN OF THE TREES
Turners Hill Road
Crawley Down
Crawley
West Sussex RH10 4HL
Tel: 0342 712536
Promotes tree planting and protection worldwide

NATIONAL SOCIETY FOR CLEAN AIR
136 North Street
Brighton
East Sussex BN1 1RG
Tel: 0273 26312
Promotes clean air through the reduction of air pollution, noise and other contaminants

OXFAM
274 Banbury Road
Oxford
OX2 7DZ
Tel 0865 56777
Third World Development issues. Posters, packs and study notes.

ROYAL SOCIETY FOR NATURE CONSERVATION
The Green
Witham Park
Lincolnshire LN5 7JR
Tel: 0522 544400
British nature conservation issues. Has contact addresses for all county (and urban) naturalists trusts. Junior Group WATCH, posters, project packs.

ROYAL SOCIETY FOR THE PREVENTION OF CRUELTY TO ANIMALS (RSPCA)
The Causeway
Horsham
West Sussex RH12 1HG
Tel: 0403 64181
Aims to prevent cruelty and to promote kindness to animals. Junior membership, posters, information packs

ROYAL SOCIETY FOR THE PROTECTION OF BIRDS (RSPB)
The Lodge
Sandy
Bedfordshire SG19 2DL
Tel: 07676 80551
Promotes conservation of wild birds. Young Ornithologists Club (YOC), posters.

SCOTTISH WILDLIFE TRUST
225 Johnston Terrace
Edinburgh EH1 2NH
Tel: 031 226 4602
Aims to conserve all forms of wildlife and habitat in Scotland.

THAMES WATER AUTHORITY
Rivers Division
Nugent House
Vastern Road
Reading
Berkshire RG1 8DB
Responsible for river operations, pollution control, fisheries, amenity and conservation.

TIDY BRITAIN GROUP
The Pier
Wigan WN3 4EX
Tel: 0941 824620
Protects and enhances the amenities of town and country. Promotes control of litter, recycling and environmental improvement schemes.

UNIVERSITIES FEDERATION FOR ANIMAL WELFARE (UFAW)
8 Hamilton Close
South Mimms
Potters Bar
Hertfordshire EN6 3QD
Tel: 0707 58202
Teaches correct methods for care and management of animals in zoos, laboratories, the wild, schools and the home.

URBAN SPACES SCHEME (USS)
Department of Food and Biological Sciences
Polytechnic of North London
Holloway Road
London N5
Tel: 071 607 2789 ext 2118
Promotes use of urban areas for ecological teaching in schools in North London.

URBAN WILDLIFE GROUP (UWG)
11 Albert Street
Birmingham
B4 7UA
Tel: 021 236 3626
Promotes conservation of natural flora and fauna in urban areas.

VEGETARIAN SOCIETY
Park Dale Road
Altringham
Cheshire WA14 4QG
Tel: 061 928 0793
Aims to improve knowledge of the health and ecological benefits of a vegetarian diet.

WARMER CAMPAIGN
83 Mount Ephraim
Tunbridge Wells
Kent TN4 8BS
Tel: 0892 24626
Campaigns for energy from rubbish

WATER AUTHORITIES ASSOCIATION
1 Queen Annes Gate
London SW1H 9BT
Tel: 071 222 8111
Concerned with water quality (both fresh and sea)

WHALE AND DOLPHIN CONSERVATION SOCIETY
20 West Lea Road
Bath
Avon BA1 3RL
Conservation and protection of whales and dolphins

WILDFOWL AND WETLANDS TRUST
The Wildfowl and Wetlands Centre
Slimbridge
Gloucestershire GL2 7BT
Tel: 045389 333
Conservation of wildfowl and their wetland habitats. Produces education resources

WOODLAND TRUST
Autumn Park
Dysart Road
Grantham
Lincolnshire NG31 6LL
Tel: 0476 74297
Aims to conserve woods and trees in the UK

A comprehensive directory of environmental organisations in Britain and Ireland is **"Directory for the Environment 1986-87"** compiled and edited by Michael J C Barker, published by Routledge & Kegan Paul.

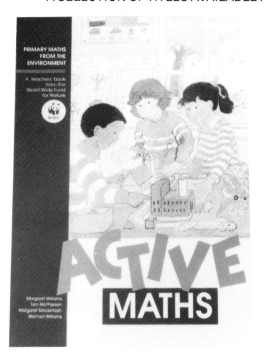

ACTIVE MATHS

Primary Maths from the Environment

Margaret Williams, Toni McPherson, Margaret Mackintosh and Michael Williams

A handbook for teachers of Mathematics at Key Stage 1, Active Maths places emphasis on enjoyment and appreciation of the environment as first steps towards an active concern for the future.

Seven themes – buildings, industrialisation and waste; climate; energy; people and their communities; plants and animals; soils, rocks and minerals; and water – provide a series of environmentally linked contexts which are realistic, meaningful and enjoyable for the learning and teaching of Mathematics.

The text has been structured to follow closely the requirements of the National Curriculum for Mathematics. Each theme provides an introduction, discussion points and a range of mathematical activities which start with play or exploration and gradually become more specific and challenging. Assessments follow the activities, and suggestions for further development through cross-curricular and home/school links are given. Each section ends with an investigation.

Teachers at all levels of experience should find the material stimulating, helpful and a good basis for continuing constructive, valuable and rewarding educational activities.

ISBN 0 947613 35 8
Price: £9.95

CATCHING THE LIGHT

A resource book for Key Stage 1 teachers on Language and the Environment

Brian Moses

Catching the Light is a manual of practical ideas for teachers of 5-8 year olds. It aims to cover aspects of language teaching with suggestions for environmentally-based work that address themselves to the requirements of the National Curriculum for English at Key Stages 1 and 2.

The book begins with the child and his/her surroundings. It then offers ideas for reading, writing, talking and listening in areas such as the home and neighbourhood, school and school environs, towns and cities, the countryside, the seashore, water and endangered animals. Details of recommended books that consider environmental issues are also given. In addition, links are made with wider issues – children in other lands, refugees, schools in the Third World, homelessness, protecting the environment, and with ecological issues such as the plight of the rainforests.

Poetry and prose by both adult writers and children is featured, linked to appropriate language activities, and there are further pointers to picture books and young fiction that might service as stimulus material.

ISBN 0 947613 30 7
Price: £8.95

LEARNING TOGETHER

Susan Fountain

Learning Together is a practical handbook for teachers of the 4-7 age group, that shows how to develop the vital social and personal skills that underlie all learning.

Fully illustrated with photographs and line-drawings, it provides a wealth of teaching ideas, practical classroom-tested activities and games designed to foster co-operation, self-esteem and communication skills. A full colour co-operative game to cut out and make is also included.

The approach is cross-curricular with a special chart indicating how the activities can be integrated into core National Curriculum work. It also provides strategies for social and personal education across the class and whole school – a blueprint for school planning and inset work.

Learning Together is published by Stanely Thornes in association with WWF UK and the Centre for Global Education, York University.

ISBN 0 7487 0439 6
Price: £6.99

For full order details and information on WWF's extensive range of education materials, write for a copy of the WWF Education Catalogue. Write to: WWF UK Education, Panda House, Weyside Park, Godalming, Surrey GU7 1XR